STARTING POINTS

WHAT EVERY TEENAGER NEEDS TO KNOW ABOUT LIFE'S

STARTING POINTS

J. DAVID SCHMIDT

OLIVER NELSON

A Division of Thomas Nelson Publishers
Nashville • Atlanta • Camden • Kansas City

ISBN 0-8407-9535-1

*Dedicated
to
my wife
Melinda*

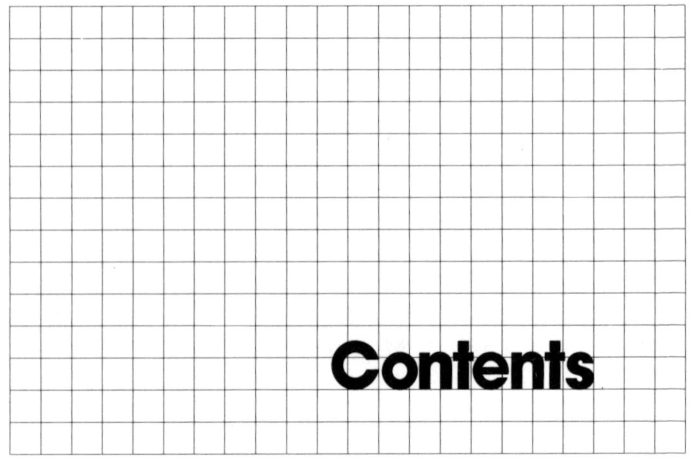

Acknowledgments / ix

1   If you want to end right, you've got
to start right / 13

2   Like it or not, God is in charge / 18

3   Knowing God personally is not an option / 27

4   The Bible is the best way to get
to know God better / 37

5   When facing a tough decision, balance
your feelings with faith / 45

6   Obeying God is better than making a lot
of sacrifices for Him / 54

7   Life comes in three colors: black,
white, and grey / 59

8 Spend more time in the safe zone,
not the grey zone / 67

9 Going to church is part of God's good plan
for your life / 75

10 Live life at the right temperature / 82

11 God is more interested in you becoming
a whole person than He is in
you being comfortable / 88

12 To be a winner in life, you've got
to have self-control / 97

13 Believe in yourself the same way
God believes in you / 104

14 Develop God's sense of timing
in your life / 112

15 Have courage to speak up for Christ / 122

16 There is always hope, even when
life turns ugly / 130

17 Be careful what sexual baggage
you pick up / 139

18 Tell the truth in everything / 152

19 Remember, things that count come before
having style / 161

20 Hold loosely to things in your life / 169

21 You CAN make a difference! / 176

22 You'll gain your life by losing it / 183

Conclusion / 189

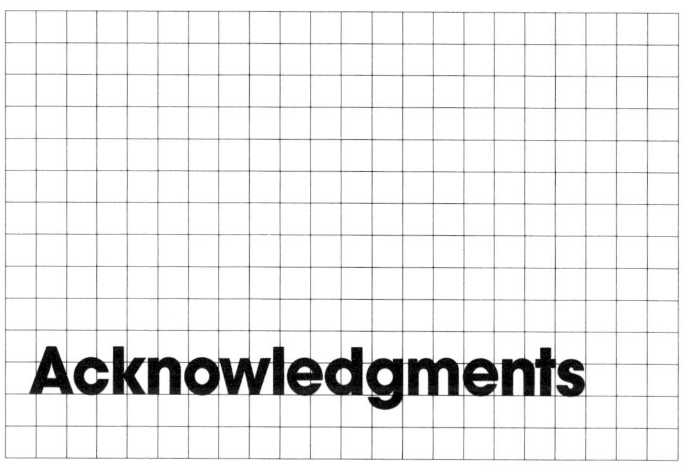

A special thank you *to my friends,*
Victor Oliver, John Gration, Bill Jefferson,
and Paul Robbins,
and *to my parents,*
for demonstrating in their lives
the possibility of being a friend of God's.

STARTING POINTS

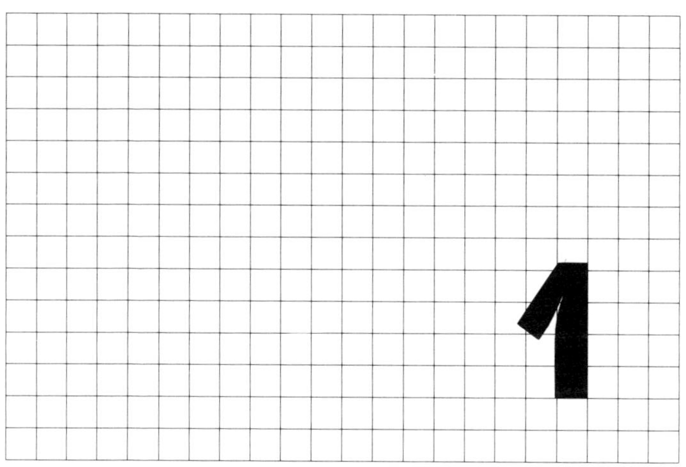

Did you ever walk up to the front door of your local convenience store and see this big, yellow and black sign plastered across the front door?

> **NO SHOES**
> **NO SHIRT**
> **NO SERVICE**

And then, hanging right beside that sign, another one says:

> **ONLY 6 STUDENTS ALLOWED IN THE STORE AT ONE TIME.**

One thing is for sure. Those signs weren't put there for your grandmother! There's only one group of people those signs are hung there for. You've got it . . . you and all your friends! And the owner means business. If you enjoy the simple things in life, like breathing, you'll do what the sign says.

This book has a lot to do with signs like No shoes, No shirt, No service. Only, instead of the signs in your local 7-Eleven, this book is about some important signs that have been hung to help you through life.

The signs we are going to see are special, because these signs have been hung by God—with *you* in mind.

- Maybe you've lost your way recently and have been trying to figure your life out.
- Maybe you need a new start. Lots of people make mistakes and just want to start over.
- Maybe you're just getting started with your life and want to know more about God and what He has to say about getting the most out of life.

These signs are for you. We'll call them *starting points*, because they'll tell you how to have a good start in life and how to start over when you've blown it. They'll tell you how to get to first base. And that's really super important because there's something you need to know. Here it is:

STARTING POINT 1

If you want to end right, you've got to start right.

Have you ever gotten bummed because you had a bad start at something? You get in the car and turn on the radio just in time to hear the last half of your favorite song. Or, what about sports that demand a perfect start, like swimming or the long jump? If your start is bad, you can hang up *that* effort.

Here's something worse. What if you start a conversation with someone you like in the hall—but you start with the wrong words?! You know the feeling. You try to sound normal, but inside you're getting weaker by the second. You sound like a frog with laryngitis every time you open your mouth. You turn red. You're about to get sick in front of your locker. The person thinks you're a nerd, and you know it. If you could get your locker open, you'd crawl inside. And all because the first thing you said came out very uncool.

Well, life's the same. If you start with a bad way of thinking, you're going to find yourself in trouble somewhere along the way. If bad starts only affected things like whether you win a swimming race or whether you go out on a date, life wouldn't be so bad. But the fact is, the wrong starting point can affect you in more significant ways. If a girl gets pregnant, a guy puts a bullet in his head, or you waste your life by not making something of it, it has a lot more to do with starting wrong than with finishing wrong.

Helping you get the basics right is what this book is all about, and getting the basics right will help you have a good start in a lot of important areas.

You have your whole life ahead of you. You have lots of choices: where you go to school, how much money you'll make, what career you will have, whom you'll marry, where you'll live, and what kind of car you'll drive. And you face more important choices, too. Who will God be to you? How will you treat your friends and your family? All of these choices face you.

Frankly, you're going to need some help. The best place to go for this help is the Bible. There is no better book in the world to help you through life. Scattered throughout the Bible are lots of signs. Lots of starting points. Good solid ideas to help you sort out what some of your friends say and what God says is the best way to handle life's challenges.

Jesus told a story about two men. One man built a house on a rock. Another man built a house on the sand. It started to rain one day, and the water of a nearby stream rose. The winds blew like crazy. When it finally quit thundering and lightning, and when the winds died down, only one house was left—the one built on the rock. If you've ever been on the beach when the tide came in, you know what happened to the house built on sand.

Hey, if you want to build your life on a rock rather than sand, check out the rest of God's starting points. See what God's been up to and what signs He's been hanging. Pick a chapter and read it. **You'll** soon **see that God's starting points make an awful lot of sense.**

God-shrinkers are everywhere. You can't spot them by the way they walk, but you sure can by the way they talk. God-shrinkers might have good jobs, be totally hip, or even turn their library books in on time. But for all their cool, God-shrinkers can look awfully dumb sometimes. They say things like "No one ever saw God," "I can't feel God," "I never hear God's voice, so there must not be a God." God-shrinkers might be very bright people, but they're not very smart. Someone needs to say to the God-shrinkers of the world, "Come to the party."

Twenty years ago, many scientists and college professors were sure God was dead or that He never existed in the first place. Today, things are different. The more knowledgeable scientists and people become, and the more sophisticated their abilities to probe the universe with telescopes and satellites, the closer they come to the conclusion that the universe started someplace and more likely with Someone.

Your science teacher might not talk about it, but some very smart people find it difficult to believe that we are all here by a random set of circumstances.

How do you feel about God? If you talked to your friends, you'd discover something interesting. Nearly everyone has some sense of God. What about you? Have you ever felt God? Maybe you felt God when you fell in love, walked in the woods alone, or slept under the stars one night. Maybe you can't explain it, but you felt "something."

If you were to take a tape recorder out on the street and ask people what they feel about God, you might get things like: "He's a mean old man in the sky who's out to get you." Or, "God and nature are the same." Or, "God is terribly weak because He let Hitler kill six million Jews." Those responses are from God-shrinkers. When people can't experience God or prove He really exists, they shrink Him. The fact is, God defies their description.

You've probably met your share of God-shrinkers. If they come across something they can't explain or that doesn't feel good, they start rationalizing. All around you in school are people who say, "Oh, you use God as a crutch." Or, "People believe in God out of fear." These statements are basically cop-outs. People make these statements because they are uncomfortable with the concept of God. Their starting point is wrong.

Eventually, every person in your homeroom, every person in your family, all your friends, and you have to answer a very important question: Do you believe God is in charge?

Everything you do in life is colored by how you answer that question. A lot of people, and maybe even you, aren't comfortable with the idea of God. But that doesn't change this starting point:

STARTING POINT 2

Like it or not, God is in charge.

God. The Chief Executive Officer in charge of the whole universe. El Presidente. Head Coach, Humanity's first and best friend.

Talk about starting points! There really is no other place to start than with God. If you have trouble with this starting point, you are going to have trouble with all the rest, because everything about being Christian hangs on this one.

If you don't believe that God is in charge, then you have to deal with something very unpleasant—the notion that you live in a random chance universe, that what happens to you, what kind of job you get, and what state of health you enjoy are all based on some random throw of the dice. A random world makes you 100 percent dependent on circumstances in your family, your education and choice of schools, and your own abilities. And if there's no order to this world, then there's no reason for you to be here and no hope for your future. And here's something to think about: No hope means you die, you go in the ground, and that's it.

In biology you learn that nature is filled with a lot of organization and detail. The kind of organization in a maple tree or the food chain in the ocean is pretty tough to explain outside of God. And what are scientists saying these days about the origin of the universe? They know that the universe is basically spreading apart, rushing away *from* some point. So, if you run time backwards, everything in the universe would be rushing *to* something. To one common source. To one common beginning. And that common source and beginning has to be God.

You can look at nature and the stars forever. You can listen to different philosophers and hear what they say about God. But the greatest proof—and the one that is toughest to argue with—is that when people believe in God and let Him be in charge, their lives change. Something good happens. People who were creeps, murderers, liars, failures in school, or dopers turn their life around and do something that counts when they let God be in charge. Maybe you already believe God is in charge or want to.

How in the world do you even get to God? You can't see Him or hear Him. So where in the world is He?

Many people say they have the true pathway to God. Some say, "Join our small group," and you end up playing Dungeons and Dragons. Some people say the way to experience God is to pop pills or maybe even worship the devil. A lot of cults say they know the pathway to God. You've got to watch out for them, because their so-called path to God will take you in the opposite direction.

Others may say you have to join their church to find the real pathway to God.

Perhaps the most confusing people who claim to know the pathway to God are those who already believe in God. Some of them say the pathway to God is to be super religious or to have a certain kind of religious experience like talking in a strange language. Some others say not going to the movies or not listening to rock music is the pathway to God.

Now here is something you need to think about. *When anybody says you have to join a certain cult or a specific church, or that you must be super religious to find God, stop and think.* Whether a Mormon, a Moonie, a Mennonite, or a Methodist, that person is all wrong to tell you he or she has the only pathway to God *if Jesus is left out.*

The truth is, there *is* only one true path to God—

the path that goes right through the most famous person in history, Jesus Christ. Any time you talk about God, you've got to talk about Jesus. That's because God and Jesus are the same.

Does that sound confusing? It does to me, too. But here's the scoop. Way back in the beginning of time, people messed up. (Remember Adam and Eve and the Garden of Eden?) God hated that because until then, God and Adam and Eve had been super tight, taking walks together and everything. More than that, though, God got lonely. That's right. The Creator of the universe got lonely. God had created people for His friendship, and they had disobeyed Him. The result was that Adam and Eve separated themselves and all of their descendants from God.

So God set up this rather intricate system of animal sacrifices, special holidays, and church services that would help people focus on God and remember He was in charge. That system sort of worked and sort of didn't. People kept right on living the way they wanted to, acting like God wasn't in charge of anything.

So God, patiently trying to help, let that go on for almost three thousand years. And then God put in motion a plan He had been working on for a long time. Now here's the mystery—the tricky part that's hard to understand. God made a decision that one major perfect sacrifice, one huge special one, would clear everything up and make it possible for us to have a close friendship with Him again.

The sacrifice God chose was His own Son. You got it. Jesus Christ. So God sent Jesus in a supernatural way to earth in the form of a man (that's the whole meaning of Christmas) to bridge the gap between Himself and us.

You know what? God's plan worked. Jesus came. He taught us how to live. He lived a perfect life. He was killed by people who hated Him. But here's the best part, even though it's a little hard to fully understand. Jesus died, but God helped Him come back to life. By doing that, Jesus overcame death—which is God's biggest enemy, because God never intended us to die. And because Jesus overcame death, anyone who has faith and believes in Him can live forever. And God did all of this because He cares about you and everyone who ever lived. Some kind of incredible story, isn't it? That's the way God is. Incredible. Always in control of the whole universe. Doing what's best for us.

One book, the Bible, has a lot to say about God. Keep in mind now, a lot of religions in the world claim to have a special book that talks about their religion. But only one book, the Bible, claims to be *the very words of the one true God.* That makes the Bible worth looking at, since God says what's in the Bible are His thoughts. Here's one of them:

Can you fathom the mysteries of God? Can you prove the limits of the Almighty? They are higher than the heavens—what can you do? They are deeper than the depths of the grave—What can you know? Their measure is longer than the earth and wider than the sea.

—JOB 11:7–9 NIV

Or try this one:

Who has understood the spirit of the LORD, or instructed him as his counselor? Whom did the Lord consult to enlighten him; and who taught Him the right way? Who was it that taught him knowledge or showed him the path of understanding? Sure the nations are like a drop in a bucket; they are regarded as dust on the scales; He weighs the islands as though they were fine dust. . . . "To whom will you compare me? Or who is my equal?" says the Holy One. Lift your eyes and look to the heavens: Who created all these? He who brings out the starry host one by one, and calls them each by name. Because of his great power and mighty strength, not one of them is missing. . . . Do you not know? Have you not heard? The Lord is the everlasting God, the Creator of the ends of the earth. He will not grow tired or weary, and His understanding no one can fathom. He gives strength to the weary and increases the power of the weak. Even youths grow tired and weary, and young men stumble and fall; but those who hope in the LORD will renew their strength. They will soar on wings like eagles; they will run and not grow weary, they will walk and not be faint.

—ISAIAH 40:13–40 NIV

Those thoughts say no one taught God what He knows! No one can describe Him completely. No one compares to God. He has more power than all the atom bombs put together that have ever been made or will be made. *God is the ultimate starting point for everything in the universe.*

Sometimes people forget that God has always been alive and that He is so smart that no one can understand how smart He is. God decides how hot and cold it will be, who gets to be king, even when the world will come to an end. He started history and put it all in motion. You and other people your age might grow tired and forget that God is in charge. But when you put your hope in God, your life changes, your strength is renewed, and you are able to fly through life with wings like eagles.

One final thought: The key to being truly free in your life is to let God be God and be in charge. Maybe your friends are God-shrinkers because they can't handle how big God is.

Accept the fact that God is in charge. If you do, you'll find a new freedom and be able to experience God in a way you never thought was possible.

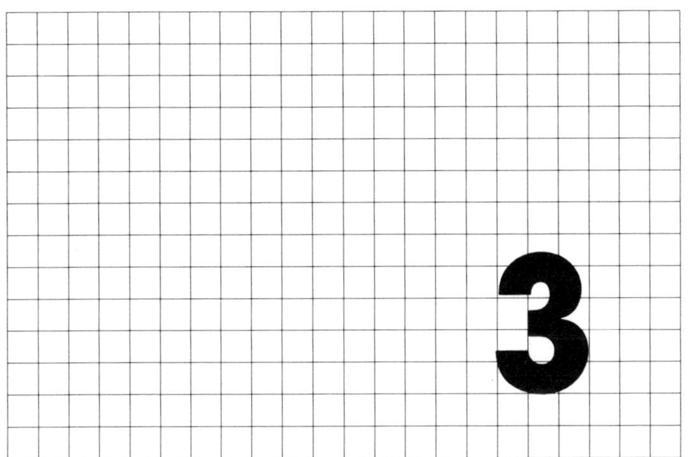

Picture yourself in church on a hot Sunday morning in the middle of summer. Your minister has just started the closing song. You're dying inside! Just as soon as this song is over you're out of there and home for some quick lunch then over to Karen's house. Man, what a girl! Nobody kisses . . . oh, yeah, back to church. What's the preacher saying? "Are you Saved?" "Have you been born again?" "Have you accepted Christ?" "Have you invited Jesus into your heart?" Wow! What a string of questions.

If you grew up in a church, you might be tempted to skip over any talk about being a Christian. You've probably heard a lot of talk about this experience. Besides, it's confusing sometimes, isn't it? Christians use twenty different ways to describe it.

Well, if you know God personally, you know that being Christian refers to a real event or process in your life. It's something that changes the way you think and live. That makes this next starting point important to you:

S T A R T I N G   P O I N T   3

Knowing God personally is not an option.

Your friends can give you some good reasons why knowing God personally is optional. If things are going your way, someone may say, "What do you need God for anyway?" Maybe you're going out on dates, have a little bit of money in your pocket, and your home life is bearable. When things are good, it's pretty hard to feel like you need God.

Maybe someone else says, "This is a Christian country—why do you have to decide to be one if you're born here?" Or your father says, "Your mother and I are Christians—that makes you one, too."

All of these sound good. There's just one small problem. None of them are true. If you are going to experience God's power and presence in your life, you will have to make a decision to do that.

God will never force you to be His friend; the choice is always up to you. Jesus said something interesting once about this. He said you have to choose a narrow path or a broad road. You'll find a lot of people on the wide road. It leads *away* from God and is the easy way to go because it's the path of least resistance. That's why your friends can drink, have sex, and lie to their parents and get away with it. It's easier to choose to do those things than to do things God's way.

When you took your driver's test, the officer probably made you drive through a winding course or between two white lines that were close together. Knowing God personally is like that. It's not like driving on a four-lane highway where, if you change lanes, it's not nearly so dangerous or difficult as it would be to pass on a one-lane road. Jesus said the decision to know God personally is a choice between a four-lane highway and a narrow road.

The Bible has something good to say about why you need to make a choice about which road you're going to be on in life.

> He [Jesus] is the image of the invisible God, the firstborn over all creation. For by him all things were created: things in heaven and on earth, visible and invisible, whether thrones or powers or rulers or authorities; all things were created by

him and for him. He is before all things, and in him all things hold together. . . . For God was pleased to have all his fullness dwell in him, and through him to reconcile to himself all things, whether things on earth or things in heaven, by making peace through his blood, shed on the cross.

—COLOSSIANS 1:15–20 NIV

Those verses mean something to you as a teenager. If you go back and read them again, you'll see that God, Jesus, really created everything in the world. It was God who came up with the idea of sex, good times, pizza, love, the beach, vacations—you name it. From the very start, God had in mind to produce beautiful things in life; but they've been produced for a reason. The biggest reason was so that in everything—from pizza and good sex to mountains and the beach—you would see God's handiwork and respect Him and thank Him for them.

But something's wrong. Look at that last verse. It says, "For God was pleased to have all his fullness dwell in him [Jesus], and through him to reconcile to himself all things, whether things on earth or things in heaven, by making peace through his blood shed on the cross."

Now, those verses imply something about you and your world. You know from Genesis that Adam and Eve messed up in the Garden of Eden. So God set up this system of laws and sacrifices to get people to think about Him. These verses say that ever since the beginning, people have never been right in their relationship with God.

Maybe you take it so casually that you don't think you really need to know God personally. If you do, it's understandable. Most of your friends in school don't take knowing God seriously. But that doesn't make them or you right—or make it not matter. Here's why. Look at what the Bible says about why it's important to know God:

> Once you were alienated from God and were enemies in your minds because of your evil behavior. But now he [God] has reconciled you by Christ's physical body through death to present you holy in his sight, without blemish and free from accusation—if you continue in your faith, established and firm, not moved from the hope held out in the gospel. This is the gospel that you heard and that has been proclaimed to every creature under heaven, and of which I, Paul, have become a servant.
>
> —COLOSSIANS 1:21–23 NIV

There it is, right in print. If you don't walk with God you're cut off from Him, because your behavior—the way you live each day—doesn't measure up to God's ways of doing things.

God did something about making it possible for you to get back to Him, though. "For God loved the world [you] so much that he gave his only Son [Jesus] so that anyone who believes in him shall not perish [have a lousy life here and die and go to hell] but have eternal life [starting the moment you believe]" (John 3:16 TLB).

God sent Jesus (remember in the last chapter we talked about that). Now, Christians talk about Jesus Christ being both man and God, and they act as though everybody should just believe it without ever asking any questions. Is that tough for you sometimes? It's tough for a lot of people to accept. How Mary ever became pregnant with a baby that was both God and man is a mystery that will stand for ever and ever. But it's part of being a Christian, though, to believe it and take it in faith.

Numerous attempts have been made down through history to show that Jesus wasn't really born to Mary and that He wasn't really God. None of them have ever stuck. A lot of smart people have dissected the whole story of Jesus Christ and who He was. Their conclusion? *The accounts in the Bible about Jesus are reliable history.* Tons of evidence show that the birth of Jesus, His life, and His death actually occurred in history.

What you believe about Jesus Christ is really up to you—it's a personal response. There have been more people throughout history who simply chose not to believe in Christ than people who investigated Christ and decided there wasn't enough proof He really was the Son of God. Did you get that? *The people who don't come to Christ are more often people who simply don't want to believe.* That brings it all back to you.

Knowing God personally means accepting (using faith to believe) who Jesus is and what He did for you. It means admitting you're not perfect (you fall short of God's laws) and that on your own, your choices won't always be what's best for you and others.

Becoming a Christian is a commitment to live life differently. It means committing yourself to live it by the guidelines in the Bible. Becoming a Christian is a step of faith, believing that Jesus Christ did something for you that you couldn't do for yourself. He paid a price by dying and rising again. His sacrifice was the ultimate God required so that anyone born after Christ, who made a choice to walk with Him, would be able to experience God's power and know Him in a personal way.

Watch out though. Being a Christian is not measured by what you do or don't do. Singing in the choir or not going all the way with your date—basically not messing up—doesn't make you a Christian. You have probably seen people who make big commitments to God, but never really follow through on them.

Being a Christian isn't a casual acquaintance with God. It's not an occasional prayer in church or devotions once or twice a month. It's not a one-way ticket out of hell. It's a new way of life for you because you admitted your guilt before God. You said to Him, "God, I mess up on my own." It's using faith to believe that Jesus is the Son of God. It's having all your past mistakes completely taken out of God's memory. It's a whole new start for you.

If you invite God into your life, He actually will come in. Some people call this "getting saved" or "being born again" or simply "becoming a Christian." **Whatever you call this experience, and wherever or however it happens, your decision to be a follower and friend of God is the most important decision you will ever make.**

With God in your life, you'll get His help to overcome problems. Maybe you feel guilty because you've tried for a long time to quit masturbating, picking up dirty magazines, lying to your parents, or eating too much. When you know God personally, you can rely on Him to help you to break bad habits or win over sins that trouble you. Having God's presence and power in your life helps you do the right thing and be free from feeling guilt.

With God in your life, you'll get His help to win over fear, too. You and God make up a team that can't be beaten. When you have to baby-sit your little brother at night, face a college entrance exam, or drive alone, God promised to be right there with you. That means you can count on Him never to leave you alone—not even for one millisecond.

With God in your life, you'll get His help to handle tough questions. A lot of people in your school may say it doesn't matter what you believe or how you live so long as you don't hurt anybody else. Who can do that, though? In our country, nobody can make a decision without eventually touching someone else (try running a red light and see what happens).

People who say whatever you do is okay if you don't hurt anybody, really think small. As a Christian, you're in touch with God, and God has given you good guidelines (in the Bible) for how people should live together. You're really going back to basics, back to the source, when you walk with God.

Perhaps the best reward for knowing God personally is that you have a reason to live. In almost every high school, kids kill themselves each year. Why do they do that?

Without God, they lost hope. You won't find anybody in your whole high school who can give you a good enough reason to live, especially when things get tough. But with God in your life, there is always hope. And with God, there is hope for injustice. Good people you know die of cancer, or maybe your parents got a divorce. **Without God in your life, there is no real good explanation for the hurt and the injustice in the world. But with Him, there's hope for making that injustice go away.** Plus, God promised that all the people who ever believed and walked with Him would live forever in heaven, even if they died here on earth (yeah, another mystery, but it's really for real).

So, our starting point is simply this: Knowing God is not an option if you want to live forever and have God's help here on earth. It's something *you* must decide upon. You must come to grips with the knowledge you have about who Jesus Christ is and why He came to earth. Maybe you're in the process right now of deciding whether or not you buy into the whole game. It isn't easy—ever so many voices say ever so much. It seems easier to simply live your life casually and not hurt anybody else. That sounds like good thinking. It sounds easier than making a choice about which road you are going to take in life. But you need to know this—*the rest of your life hangs on this one question: Who is Jesus to you?* What you do with this question is up to you. Michael W. Smith says in one of his songs, it's a "lie that a heart never changes." Don't buy the lie. With God in your life, a whole new world awaits you.

Something to think about: *There's no big trip to becoming a friend of God.* It's a decision and a prayer to invite Jesus (God) into your life. Whatever you want to call the experience, it's up to you. Have you had yours yet?

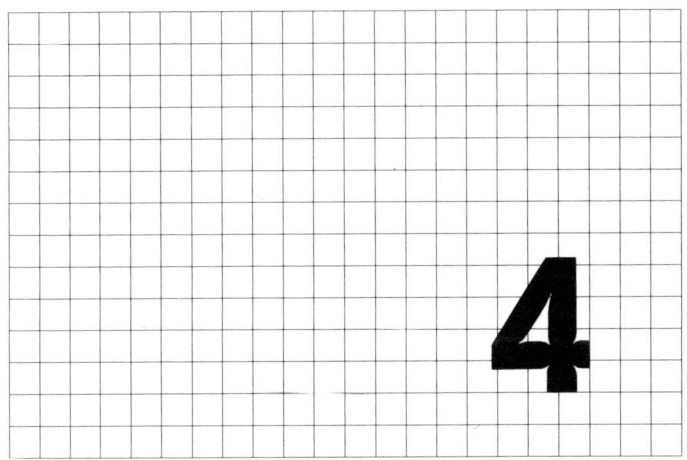

Maybe you've been in church enough to know that you should read your Bible, and so you make the big attempt. But getting through only ten verses in the Bible should win you the endurance award of the week. Sometimes you feel that you need a secret decoder ring to figure out what the Bible says. Every religious person you know calls it the Living Word. Right! If this is "living"— you'd love to see what dead is. What are you supposed to do with this book, anyway?

Some books aren't worth reading. One is. Let's talk about a good book. *The* good book: the Bible. What do you think about your Bible anyway? Hey, here's a good question—do you even know where your Bible *is* right now?

When you read your Bible, do you sometimes think it was never translated from Greek? Welcome to a large group of people who know the Bible is an important book but have trouble getting into it.

STARTING POINT 4

The Bible is the best way to get to know God better.

Isn't it odd that God would choose a book instead of, say, television to talk with you? Television would be so easy, wouldn't it? If you could see Jesus or God on TV, it would make your life much simpler, take away many of your doubts. But God chose a book. (That says something about what God really thinks about books!) Of all the times in history God could choose to share His thoughts, He picked a time when scrolls were the big way to communicate.

Some people have really weird ideas about the Bible. They won't put another book on top of it. It has to be set in a certain place. Some churches carry the Bible around in spectacular ceremonies. The fact is, nothing bad will ever happen to you if you drop your Bible or put another book on top of it. Some people put too much emphasis on the book itself. It's a special book, but not because it's leather bound on onionskin paper. It's a special book because of what it says. What you do with your Bible is up to you.

The important thing is, you get to know the One who wrote the Bible, not worship the book. Your Bible is a unique book that has some great stories, eyewitness accounts, history, personal letters, a love story, and a little poetry. (Don't sweat the history and poetry. It's not so bad as the stuff you read in school.)

The Bible records examples of how God deals with people. It shows how consistent God is. It tells how people react when good things happen and when bad things happen. It lets us know what makes God tick.

The most awesome thing about this book is that forty different people—all with different backgrounds and occupations—wrote the Bible in three different languages, and it took them more than sixteen hundred years to do it. When they were done, all 873,367 words of the Bible worked together in harmony to talk about one God, one devil, one heaven, one hell, and one way of salvation. **This book has withstood wars, criticism, and time to become the best-selling book in history. Not bad for a book that started out on scrolls, huh?**

The Bible proves you can depend on God. What He said He would do two thousand, three thousand, years ago for someone else, He'll stand behind and do for you today.

For the time in which it was written, the Bible made perfect sense. Does it still make perfect sense for you today? You bet. Sure, you have to translate some things, and that's where you might need some professional help, say from a teacher or a preacher. But after thousands of years, the Bible still hangs together. The New Testament endorses what the Old Testament says. The Old Testament predicts what happens in the New Testament.

Sometimes people say, "It's only a history book, no book could be *that* special . . . it's just ancient stories full of inconsistencies." That's something you hear often—that the Bible's inconsistent. The problem is, people try to treat the Bible like a science book. It isn't. It is a history book. It isn't designed to tell you why things are the way they are but simply to record and explain God and His ways.

The Bible demonstrates something important. God wants to be a partner with us. He had human beings write down what He said to them. As a Christian, you need to believe God controlled that process and guaranteed that exactly what He wanted said got written down. If you're looking for the Bible to be a perfect book, give it up. People aren't perfect, and people worked with God to write the Bible. They wrote down the thoughts God gave them. People who put exacting standards on the Bible—which they don't place on any other book—are usually the same people looking for a way out of believing it.

Do you ever get confused about the right thing to do in certain situations? Believing the Bible will help you right where you are in life. Do you realize that every major question you have about sex, how far to go on a date, what kind of music to listen to, parties, friendships, whom to marry, what job to get, are all addressed in the Bible? There's guidance for every major decision you'll ever face.

One place in the Bible says that God's words are full of living power and are sharper than the sharpest dagger; they cut swift and deep into your innermost thoughts and desires with all their parts exposing you for what you really are. Any book that can do that is going to help you learn to think straight.

It will help guide you to do the right thing because you're going to find out (if you read it) what God really thinks is right and wrong. Sometimes the Bible says something you don't want it to. Or maybe you feel like you can't do what it says. That's when you feel like doing a little "creative interpretation." You try to adjust it to make it fit your situation: "The Bible never said you couldn't have a butt now and then." Or, "Sure, the Bible says going all the way is wrong, but what if you stop before that?" Or, "Gossip is what other people do. I'm just talking about a former friend. The Bible can't mean that's wrong."

Adjusting the Bible simply doesn't work. You have to take what it says at face value. If your starting point is that the Bible is adjustable, you'll find that the Bible will never really come alive for you. Eventually, everything you read in it will become relative.

Once Jesus told a story about how important the Bible is to a Christian. He talked about some seeds which fell in different places. He explained His story like this:

> The seed is God's message to men. The hard path where some seed fell represents the hard hearts of those who hear the words of God, but then the devil comes and steals the words away and prevents people from believing and being saved. The stony ground represents those who enjoy listening to sermons, but somehow the message never really gets through to them and doesn't take root and grow. They know the message is true, and sort of believe it for awhile; but when the hot winds of persecution [trouble] blow, they lose interest. The seed among the thorns represents those who listen and believe God's words but whose faith afterwards is choked out by worry and riches and the responsibilities and pleasures of life. And so they are never able to help anyone else to believe the Good News. But the good soil represents honest, good-hearted people. They listen to God's words and cling to them and steadily spread them to others who also soon believe.
>
> —LUKE 8:11–15 TLB

God wants you to listen to His words, cling to them, and spread them so that His words can be of help to others, also. Jesus' story is a warning: Pleasures of life, materialism, troubles, and not really being serious about your friendship with God all can make God's word of no value to your life. God has a better idea. He wants the Bible to help you. So trust it, don't adjust it.

Amy Grant sings a song from the Bible that goes like this:

Thy Word is a lamp unto my feet . . .

Your feet probably want to go a lot of places—some good places and some not so good. A while back Wham sang a song called "Guilty Feet Have Got No Rhythm." When your feet go places they shouldn't, they lose their rhythm. The Bible can help you and guide you where you should walk in life and where you shouldn't.

and a light unto my path.

—PSALM 119:105 KJV

Let's face it. It's easy to wander off the right path in life, isn't it? To get lost? There are a lot of voices saying, "Hey, this is okay . . . it's okay to do this . . . don't worry about that. . . ." That's why God gave us His thoughts in the Bible. He wants us to know what happened to other people who faced the same problems and how He helped them.

In fact, God was pretty smart to give us His thoughts in a book. Can you imagine having to go to your computer or wait for a radio program to hear from God? With your own Bible you can hear from God anytime. The Bible can be your best companion in life.

The God that you've never seen but have only experienced in your heart and mind can speak to you through the Bible. Sometimes your Bible is going to read like a rock. That's okay. Maybe you're having a bad day and you're bummed out, or maybe there are some things in your life that have made you cold toward God.

Here's the important thing: *Never give up reading your Bible!* Even if you read a few verses a day, make a commitment to God and to yourself to read your Bible even when you don't feel like it. If you are willing to obey and listen to what is in the Bible, you are going to find it is the best book in the house.

The Bible was written to communicate with you. Put this starting point in place in your life: Trust God's Word, take it to heart. When God speaks to you while you are reading it, do what He says. You'll find the kind of help that you are looking for.

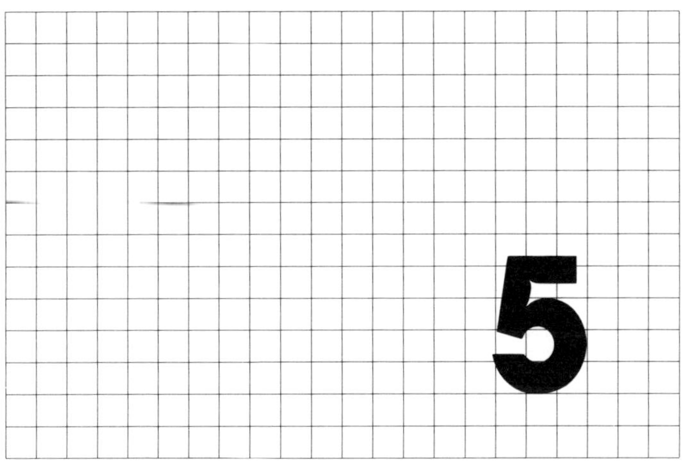

5

You walked out the door that night feeling up. You had your best jeans on and felt a little rowdy. It was your fourth date with someone you had really started to care about.

Later, on the way home, you felt a little sick inside. Okay, you didn't go all the way, but you did more than something inside told you that you should. C'mon, who wouldn't have? When you care about someone and you get a little hot, it's hard to figure out what's right and wrong. It felt right at the time. You'd never been with anyone who was willing to go that far. Sometimes it's confusing to know what to do when something feels right.

In the 1984 presidential race Geraldine Ferraro, the Democratic vice-presidential candidate, made a Coke commercial in which she told her daughters how great Coke was. In the commercial one of her daughters asked a question. Her answer was this, "If it feels right, it must be right."

Take a look at that answer. Here is a smart, intelligent, and well-informed candidate for vice president saying, "If it feels right, it must be right." Can you believe it? Do you think she really meant that? Can you imagine somebody like that for a vice president? "I felt that watching Friday night videos was right, Mr. President, that's why I didn't show up for the State Dinner." "I got angry with the Libyans, and since my anger felt right, I dropped a bomb on them." "It just felt right that the White House would look better pink."

It sounds goofy to hear someone like her say that ("If it feels right, it must be right"), but that's the way a lot of people today are making choices. If-it-feels-right-it-must-be-right thinking steers people as they make choices about having sex, using drugs, drinking, and deciding what music they listen to, what clothes they wear, what car they drive, or whether they'll study or walk with God.

What about you? If something feels right to you it must be right, right? Wrong.

STARTING POINT 5

When facing a tough decision, balance your feelings with faith.

Some choices you make in life have to be based on what you feel. For little things, making choices based on what you feel is no problem, for instance, what kind of car you drive, what toothpaste you use, what road you take to school. For some things, it really doesn't matter how you choose. Life will turn out the same.

But there are other choices—what you wear, whom you date, or when you study for a final—that can go bad for you if you choose strictly by how you feel one day.

And what about the really big decisions like sex? College? Drugs? God?

When it comes to those big things, you need more than just your feelings to go on to make good decisions. What will it be? That's where you have to put this starting point in place. You have to learn to *balance your feelings with some faith.*

Now balancing feelings with faith gives everyone problems. It is a tough area to get straight in life. But look what can happen if you don't.

If your starting point is that your feelings are the

most accurate thing to listen to, do you know what happens? You end up making bad choices and have a lot of problems. Why?

Because *sometimes your feelings aren't right.* Just because it feels right doesn't mean your feelings are accurate.

Your feelings come from inside you. They are part of your personality. They've been tuned like you'd tune a piano, by your home life, by how your parents have raised you, and by experiences you've had that shaped your conscience to sense what is right and wrong. Sometimes friends or circumstances can make you feel a certain way. Even our bodies affect our feelings. Every girl knows that. When her period comes her feelings might change quite a bit. All of these things that shape your feelings don't always help you give perfect responses.

Now, don't get me wrong. Feelings are really great; they give your life a lot of color. They're extremely important to you. They tend to reflect your real mood and what is really going on in your mind. Actually, they reflect the way you interpret life. You need your feelings to be a balanced person, whether you express how you feel fairly often or hardly ever.

But the big question is, should you trust your feelings to make decisions in life? Not very often. Frankly, if you are going to make good decisions in life you are going to have to balance your feelings with your faith in Jesus Christ. That means stopping long enough to think what Jesus Christ might tell you to do (or has already told you in the Bible) before going with how you feel.

Let's look at some really practical examples where you are going to need more than your feelings to guide you. Do you ever wake up some mornings and feel not very religious or not much like a Christian? In fact, maybe you lived two whole days and never once thought about or talked to God. What happens if you base your walk with God on your feelings? At the end of those two or three days, you may not feel very much like a Christian. Does that mean you're not a Christian?

What if you get hurt? Someone that you care about drops you or someone in your family dies. It is hard to feel God when we're hurting. Does that mean God doesn't care?

What if you don't feel God when you pray? Does that mean God doesn't hear your prayers? The answer to that question is, no way! Just because you feel a certain way doesn't mean reality changes. What you need besides your feelings is faith. Faith is an important idea to God. It's something He asks everyone who knows Him to have. Four hundred places in the Bible talk about faith—most of them talk about how faith helps us make good decisions. Here's what the Bible says about faith:

> What is faith? It is the confident assurance that something we hope for is going to happen. It is the certainty that what we hope for is waiting for us, even though we cannot see it up ahead. Men of God in days of old were famous for their faith. By faith—

by believing God—we know that the world and the stars—in fact, all things—were made at God's command; and that they were all made from things that can't be seen.

—HEBREWS 11:1–3 TLB

Let's say that you are dating this really nice person from school. You talk about everything and go out on fun dates. Sometimes you kiss a lot, sometimes other stuff. You know the Bible says what you are doing is wrong. But it doesn't *feel* wrong. What do you do? That's where you need faith to make the right decision about how far to go with somebody. There is no one standing near you when you have to make that decision; God doesn't stand there with a big club or a big warning light saying, "Don't have sex." You have to trust—have faith—that when the Bible says sex outside of marriage isn't good for you, it's the absolute truth. **Walking away from what *isn't* right, even when something *feels* right, is balancing your feelings with faith.**

Faith helps you be sure of making the right decision even when all of the signs and indicators and even your feelings tell you to go a different direction. God never meant for your feelings to be your only guide, but only to be your support in your decisions. Did your parents ever tell you to use your head for more than a hat rack? What they mean is, don't let your feelings carry you away. When faced with a decision, think. What is the *best* thing to do here?

Sometimes you may get to feeling really down in life. That is pretty normal for being a teenager. Every ninety minutes a teenager in this country commits suicide. A thousand teenagers try to kill themselves every day. Why do they do that? They feel like jerks; they break up with those they care about or something really bad happens to them. Then they act on their feelings. They feel that life is hopeless and there is no way out. So instead of having faith that God is in control, they end up killing themselves. They went with their feelings, and their feelings said there was no hope.

Now maybe you have never thought about killing yourself, but you have felt really blue and down. Or you've been afraid at night when you've been baby-sitting. Or you've felt like a real jerk at school. Or you've felt that people, and maybe even God, didn't like you.

Or maybe you're so good at something you think you're too cool to need God. Whatever your feelings about yourself, you need the real truth to balance them. It's the only way to get a true picture of reality about yourself and your world.

A guy named Noah had faith. It *felt* crazy to him to do what he did. Can you imagine building a boat like Noah did and never having seen enough rain and water to float it? Noah had to overcome his feelings. Everything inside said, "This is stupid and not very normal." But he chose to have faith, to go God's way.

You can have this kind of faith. It is choosing to

listen to the second voice inside of you that says *Stop. Don't go any further with your date.* Choose to say, "God, you help me to make this decision about which college to attend." Or, "With God's help, I will overcome what's dragging me down." That is what it means to have faith. Relying on the God you don't see and trusting the Bible's advice is best for you, though it's inconvenient, it hurts, or it isn't fun.

This starting point is very important for your life. If you insist on going with your feelings, you are going to have a fuzzy walk with God. You're never going to know quite where He is, because some days He'll feel close and other days He won't. You're going to end up making a lot of poor choices. You'll have a lousy point of view on life because you're never going to know how life is *really* going.

Every day, for the rest of your life, you'll have an abundance of choices that are going to test you as a person. You can choose to go with your feelings or choose to go with faith in God and His Word. It's all up to you. Faith may seem risky sometimes or like boring nonsense; you may *feel* like a mindless twit. But relying on God when you don't feel Him, doing the right thing when you don't feel like doing it, and believing in life even when you are down is the stuff that it takes to make it through life and to experience God's best for you.

Balancing your feelings with some faith will help you have a consistent walk with God. It will help you make good choices and save yourself a lot of hurt and pain when it comes to sex. The right person to marry. The right school to attend. You will be able to see life for what it really is.

Sure, there are a lot of momentary highs when you go with your feelings. But God has a better idea. The Bible says that *without faith it is impossible to see God.* You'll find that the more you walk by faith, the more your feelings about God and life will become accurate. Balancing your feelings with faith in God and His Word is the best way to stay out of trouble and find God's best plan for your life.

Do you get the impression sometimes that God wants to cramp your lifestyle? Jam you in such a way that you don't have any rights or freedoms? It sometimes seems to you that it's always the boring people who are Christians. Those people confuse you as to what God really wants from you.

If you went by what some Christians say, you'd believe God wants you to give up an awful lot of things in order to please Him. Do you know that the Bible says that just the *opposite* is true? That's why this next starting point is important for you to remember.

Obeying God is better than making a lot of sacrifices for Him.

It's hard to believe God doesn't want us to be religious people who give up all our money and prestige and friends to be a Christian. Some people brag about what they give up. "I never smoked a cigarette once in my life." "A can of beer has never touched my lips." "Last year I burned all my rock 'n' roll records and cassettes." "I don't go out with friends on Sunday afternoon because I'm volunteering at a nursing home." "I'm a virgin. Sort of." You know what? God doesn't give a rip about what those people give up at all. And He doesn't care what you give up in your life.

God has a different idea of what's important, and giving up a lot of things is not His first priority. Sure, God wants you to live life carefully. We've talked about ways to do that in other chapters. But what you give up isn't nearly so important to God as *how much you're obeying Him*. Why is that? Because you can't bribe God with anything. God owns everything in the whole world and universe. What could you possibly bargain with God for? "God, if I give up sex will you give me good grades?'' God doesn't need any of your bribes or anything you give up.

Sometimes Christians say, "If you give this up, God will bless you." Usually they're not talking about sin, but about things in the grey area or things *they* think you should give up. Basically, God gets very bored with our sacrifices. They don't do Him any good because He owns everything. And they don't do you much good either.

Too often, this is what happens with sacrifices. You have some short-term pain, but no real gain.

Consider what a great Jewish leader by the name of Samuel said to King Saul:

> Has the Lord as much pleasure in your burnt offerings and sacrifices as in your obedience? Obedience is far better than sacrifice. He is much more interested in your listening to him than in your offering the fat of rams to him. For rebellion is as bad as the sin of witchcraft, and stubbornness is as bad as worshiping idols.
>
> —1 SAMUEL 15:22,23 TLB

That's what God wants. He wants your obedience. He doesn't want you to be stubborn and to rebel against what He has told you is right and wrong. He wants you to obey His laws because they honor Him and because they'll protect you from a lot of pain and hurt. God wants your obedience because He has a good plan for your life, one that will bring you a lot of good times. But to find out God's plans, you've got to be willing to obey Him.

Obedience sounds like a drag, doesn't it? Maybe more than a drag, maybe it sounds like a total impossibility. Who can believe and obey everything that God wrote in the Bible? **You may not know** **_all_ of what God expects, but you can act on** **_what_ you know.** You can't obey what you're not familiar with. But right now, you do know some things that are right and wrong for you. You know what's black and white. You know that getting drunk, having sex, gossiping, losing your temper, and telling lies are wrong. God expects you to act on what you know.

Obedience is being faithful to God when it's inconvenient. It's being faithful to God when you know people will laugh at you for walking out of a dirty movie or a bad party. That's what obedience is.

God wants your friendship. He wants to hear from you when you pray. He wants to talk with you through His Word. He wants you to enjoy the gifts that He has given you on earth. And He wants you to get in the habit of consulting Him on things, because He knows you better than you know yourself. Do you realize God's ways will always be better for you than anything you could try to plan for yourself? And here's something important. _God's good will for your life is free._ You don't have to make one sacrifice for it.

Now the fact is, when you obey God you will have to make some sacrifices. But if you try to make those sacrifices before God tells you what to sacrifice, you'll end up sacrificing things God doesn't want you to sacrifice, things that are important to you. You'll miss out on some good things He's planned for you simply because you were trying to make sacrifices that weren't really important. If you don't follow this starting point, you'll end up trying to work your way into God's favor. And that's impossible.

Throughout your life, you're going to be challenged to make big sacrifices for God. Take your cues from the Bible. Ask God if it's an important sacrifice. Some are. Some aren't. God is most interested in whether you are doing what you know is right. Think about it.

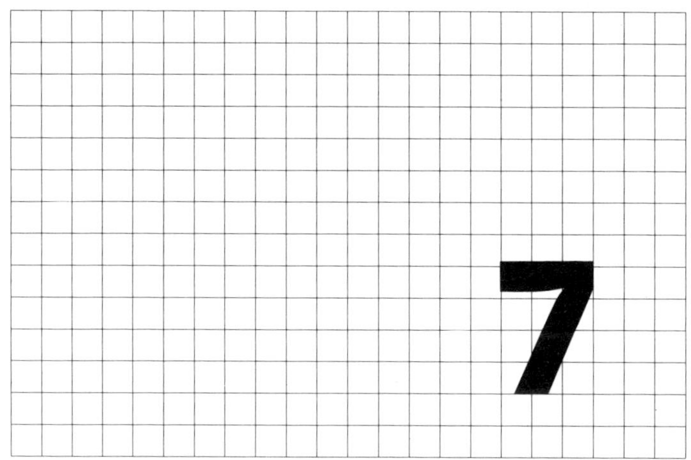

The weekend is coming up, but before you can make it to Saturday, you have to make it through two tests, a big game, and a paper—all due on the same day. Wouldn't it be great if the pressure in your life were spaced out so that you never had too much to do at one time?

Most of us like things simple in life, but the pressure at school can make life tough. There's another kind of pressure you're probably aware of, too. It's the pressure to make the right moral decisions. It's pressure because some of your friends at school will tell you, "Just do what you want to do." But some of your friends at church might say, "Hey, everything in life is black and white. See, right in the Bible it says that some

59

things are evil and some things are good." But **anybody with half a brain and who breathes air knows that life isn't always black and white. In fact, life can be downright messy sometimes.** And that leads us to this important starting point.

STARTING POINT 7

Life comes in three colors: black, white, and grey.

It would be so easy if everything in your life came in just two colors: black and white. That way you could float along and not have to make any tough decisions.

Well, this starting point is sort of a good news–bad news joke. The good news is some things in life *are* black and white. According to God, there *is* a right and a wrong way to live. There *are* black and white things in the Bible we could say are absolutely right and wrong. These are things God says you cannot do and call yourself a Christian. If you do these things, your friendship with God will be broken and you will hurt yourself.

In one place the Bible says, "Don't fool yourselves. Those who live immoral lives, who are idol worshipers, adulterers or homosexuals—will have no share in his Kingdom, neither will thieves or greedy people, drunkards, slanderers, or robbers" (1 Corinthians 6:9–10 TLB).

In another place the Bible lists seven things God hates, things like having pride, telling lies, murdering, scheming, and being a troublemaker. (See Proverbs 6:16–19.) These are pretty straightforward lists—black and white, like expanded versions of the Ten Commandments.

God gave us these lists because He knows we are basically weak inside—and not always interested in going His way in life. That means our attitudes and actions separate us from Him.

Nowadays, we don't like to talk about sin. Some psychologists say sin is a concept that hurts people. But the Bible makes it clear that sin is a real thing that separates us from God. Sin means we are not pleasing God by what we say, think, or do. Sin is a real condition in every living person. It happens in your life, your preacher's life, and in your parents' life. Sin is an inner desire to go your own way, not God's. When you give in to sin, there are often difficult and ugly consequences. People get hurt, and your friendship with God is broken.

But when you know God personally, you also have an inner voice calling you to do good—a voice telling you more to do right and good things than not to do wrong and bad things. Hundreds of good commands are in the Bible, but check out these absolutely good things God said to do:

- "Do for others what you want them to do for you" (Matthew 7:12 TLB).
- "Think about things that are pure and lovely, and dwell on the fine, good things in others" (Philippians 4:8 TLB).
- "Let love be your greatest aim" (1 Corinthians 14:1 TLB).
- "Let everyone bless God and sing his praises for he holds our lives in his hands" (Psalm 66:8 TLB).

In the same way, God talks to you (His Spirit talking to your spirit) warning you not to do certain things that He hates. He encourages you to do what is right.

Now, that is all basically easy enough, isn't it? There are *real* black and white things in life. But then there is that third color, that in-between color. The color grey. And that is where things get messy.

Grey is everything you enjoy doing in life that isn't specifically talked about in the Bible and that somehow you can't decide whether it is right or wrong. Grey depends a lot on whom you talk to or the situation. You'll find one person who says it is wrong and another person who says it isn't wrong. Sometimes it depends on where you live.

Grey depends a lot on your family (what they tell you is right and wrong) and what church you attend. Some churches teach that certain things are okay while other churches teach that those same things are wrong.

Twenty or thirty years ago, many Christians felt it was wrong to go to the movies in a theater. There are still Christians who feel that way today. But now, life is a little messier. The same movies that are shown in the theater you can get on cable TV in your own home.

Time has a way of changing what used to be dead wrong. Things like rock 'n' roll, movies, dancing, and playing cards were considered "sin" for people your grandparents' age. But today, some Christians feel comfortable with these things. Others don't. Many Christians still have questions about dancing, rock 'n' roll, watching TV on Sunday, covering for a friend with a white lie, smoking, or having a beer. Some Christians would say if you did any of these things that you wouldn't really be separated from the world's bad influences. You wouldn't be living a pure life.

On the other side, though, some Christians are saying, "Get hip, there's nothing wrong with going dancing on a Friday night, grabbing your date wherever you want, watching TV on Sunday, or even having a beer as long as you don't get drunk." A lot of people say to just cool out on some of this stuff.

Now, listen to this. Both of those types of people have a problem. The first group, the uptight Christians, are adding to God's Word. They're making a list of things they consider pleasing to God that is longer than the list He Himself made. They try to keep everyone secure by building tall fences and telling people not to leap over them.

On the other hand, the second group, the footloose Christians, aren't as careful as they ought to be about their lifestyle and pleasing God. They look at having their freedom as more important than protecting their walk with God.

See the problem? Neither group is really taking God at His word.

Stop the presses!

God doesn't intend His people—you—to end up thinking like either one of these groups of Christians. God doesn't want you to. In fact, He has forbidden that anyone should add to what He considers to be black and white. Only God can say what is sin. We can't; we *are* sinful, so we can't think straight about sin without God's help.

So what's the answer? Here it is. *You have to grow up and decide these things for yourself.* The decisions about what is right or wrong for you are decisions that *you* have to make.

While you live at home, you may have to live with the rules and guidelines your parents have given you. That is part of honoring your parents and is something that the Bible has commanded you to do. But when you are on your own, you're going to have to make some of these decisions for yourself. And there are risks both ways.

If you try to avoid all the things that are in the grey area of life, you'll feel quite safe that you are making the right decisions. But you may find that life will be quite boring, too. On the other hand, it's risky business to do everything that God did not necessarily say no on. You run a high risk of hurting yourself, other people, and the Lord.

What's the solution? Well, it comes out looking like this:

- Accept the fact that life does come in three colors. That's part of growing up, becoming an adult. It is an immature way to live life if you believe all decisions are easy, as if they are all black and white.
- Don't add things to God's Word that God never said were right and wrong.
- Get to know God's black and white. That's what Amy Grant's song from the psalm means: "Thy Word is a lamp unto my feet, and a light unto my path." You need to know what is black and white in God's eyes and accept the absolutes that God laid down.

There will always be decisions in life that will be grey for you. And on those things, you'll have to make up your mind. The safest way to make those decisions is to take them to God.

Ask God if you ought to be dancing, if it's right for you to masturbate, if one beer is okay for you. If you ask Him for guidance and *really* want His *best* answer for you, God will steer you in the right direction. Talk it over with your parents, your pastor, your Sunday school teacher.

There is no formula for walking with God. In God's Word, He has told us what He wants from us. He told us these things so that we would bring honor to Him. He's laid down laws, black and white rules, for us to follow for our good and also for the good of everyone around us.

But where you live, the church you go to, and the family you've grown up in have a lot to do with other areas of your life that are grey. That means you have to decide *with God's help* what is best for you.

What color are you going to live life? Live like you want, and you'll miss out on every good thing God has for you. Spend too much time living in the grey, and you'll have trouble in your life. God will seem far away. Live too uptight, and you'll never enjoy the benefits of knowing God and being friends with Him.

But live by the Book and on the grey issues ask God for guidance, and life will be a lot easier. He'll help you pick the right color to live in.

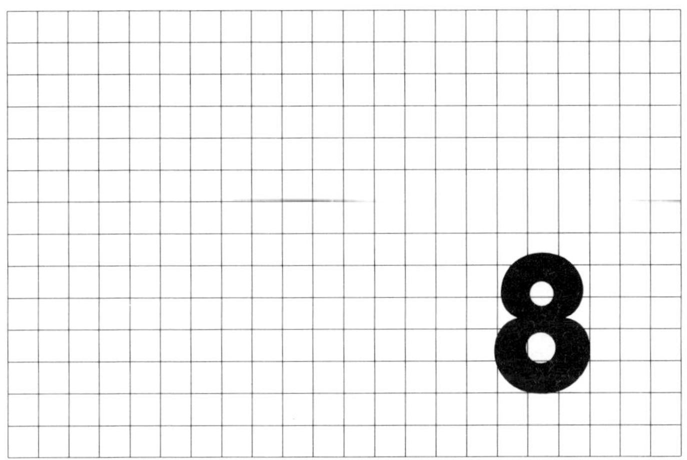

Have you ever had a week like this? You go to church on Sunday and in youth group and the sermon you hear some things that are really helpful to you. Man, you're fired up—you want to walk with God the whole week. Monday comes and you have your devotions. Nothing strikes you particularly. Tuesday comes along and you sleep in, and so you don't get a chance to read the Bible and pray. Wednesday you're running late again, and so you listen to rock 'n' roll as you hurry to get dressed. Thursday, same thing. Friday, you breathe a quick prayer then head for school early to attend a club meeting. Friday night you go out with some friends. Everybody votes to see an 'R'-rated movie. You know you probably wouldn't choose to go to it on your own. You also know your parents would give you grief if they knew you

went. But you go anyway. Saturday night your parents go out, and some friends come over and offer you a "joint."

Right now, what do you think the chances are you'll smoke that joint?

Some voice way in the back of your mind says, *Hey, you shouldn't do that.* But all your friends have smoked joints and gotten away with it in the past, and they really enjoyed it. Inside you struggle. You can't believe you're arguing with yourself. Man you're a Christian. You know better. But you struggle anyway. Who would care at that moment if you tried the joint?

Suddenly you realize you've got a problem. Your sensitivity to God's voice is dull. In fact, you're having a hard time hearing the right thing to do. What made God's voice dull? Was it the missed devotions? The rock 'n' roll music you listened to? The R-rated movie? While it would be hard to point to any one thing as the only reason, there's got to be another answer. What is it?

STARTING POINT 8

Spend more time in the safe zone, not the grey zone.

In the last chapter we talked about life coming in three colors—black, white, and grey. In many respects, living in a black and white world is easy. It's safe. You know what's right and wrong when you read the Bible. God made lists and put them right in the Bible for you to read. You know you're wrong when you go against those lists or when God speaks to you.

But some decisions you face are grey ones. (We talked about how to handle those in the last chapter.) The big question is, how much of your life can you spend living in the grey zone? Too much time in the grey zone dulls your sensitivity to God's voice and sets you up for making a big mistake. Too little time in the grey zone is unrealistic.

Generally speaking, people don't mess up their lives in one decision. A series of decisions gets a girl pregnant, makes you try a joint, or causes you to quit walking with God. Let's look at it another way. Do you ever notice that when you get in the car, you feel like you have to have the radio on? There's nothing wrong with rock 'n' roll music in and of itself, but when that's all you listen to, and God never gets a chance to speak to you, then it becomes a problem.

It's the same with having a beer or looking at a dirty magazine. It's those things you say to convince yourself—"Oh, I'll just do this once," or "I don't make a regular habit of it, but this is alright"—that dull your walk with God. It's a mystery, but somehow one beer or one look in a *Playboy* or one instance of going further than you should on a date quickens your appetite for those things. And it makes it easier for you to slip away from activities you know are black and white into activities that are grey, where you're not sure anymore.

Like drugs. So many kids—normal, regular kids who have a lot going for them in life—start by smoking a joint or getting drunk on the weekends just to get high. But something happens. Each time they use drugs or booze to get high, they end up coming down a little lower than where they started. Next time they get high, they don't get *as* high, and they end up coming down a little lower than where they started. On and on it goes until eventually these same normal, regular kids have to use booze or drugs just to feel normal.

This process can happen in any area of your life if too many times you say okay to something in the grey.

Now, this is important. **The *accumulation* of**

doing and thinking things in the grey area of life is what gets you in trouble. One time may not be bad, but it's one night of rock 'n' roll music tied to another, attached to an R-rated movie, followed by one beer that dulls your sensitivity to God.

Does that mean you can't have fun in life, you can't listen to rock 'n' roll, and you can't go to the movies? No. That means you've got to have some balance. That's where God comes into the picture. Why do you think God gave you all those desires to have fun, be with your friends, and have sex? God gave those desires to you because He wanted to give your life some fun and color and beauty. But He also wants you to handle those things very carefully, to live the bulk of your life, not in the grey zone, but in the black and white zone—the safe zone.

Paul, the traveling statesman for God, wrote some helpful thoughts for how to do this:

> Be very careful then, how you live—not as unwise but as wise, making the most of every opportunity, because the days are evil. Therefore do not be foolish, but understand what the Lord's will is.
>
> —EPHESIANS 5:15–17 NIV

> So then, dear friends, since you are looking forward to this [the day that Christ comes back to earth], make every effort to be found spotless, blameless and at peace with him. . . . be on your guard so that you may not be carried away by the

error of lawless men and fall from your secure position. But grow in the grace and knowledge of our Lord and Savior Jesus Christ.

—2 PETER 3:14,17,18 NIV

Now, *there* are a lot of clues on how to live life in the safe zone. Look at them. Be very careful how you live. Make the most of every opportunity. Don't be foolish. Understand what the Lord's will is. Make every effort to be found spotless. Be on your guard. Grow in your understanding of God. All of those things are *action* kind of things. They say, in two words, *be careful*.

If you live your life more in the grey zone than in the safe zone, you're going to find yourself getting burned, making mistakes, hurting others, and disappointing God. The answer is to be careful how you live, get to know God, get to know His Word. Like we said in the last chapter, if you want to learn to make good decisions you've got to know the Man, the One who set up the rules—and that takes reading your Bible, praying to God, and going to church where you'll get to know Him better.

Okay, here are some final thoughts. Do you know that horrible, gross feeling you have when you've made a mistake in life? Maybe you had a car accident, had sex, or told a lie. Maybe that sick feeling didn't go away for hours or days or even weeks. That was guilt, and God put guilt there as a means to warn you not to do those things again. Do you know that if you spend too much of your life living in the grey zone your sense of guilt will wear off? Then trying to make the right decision will get tougher and tougher.

When you came to know God personally, He took away all the excess baggage in your life. He made it so that you could run light in life, so that you wouldn't have to carry heavy loads of guilt and past memories and bad decisions with you. That's what Christ did at Calvary for you. He made it possible for you to be a free person. But every hour you live in the grey zone, you pick up a piece of baggage. Soon, you'll be carrying pieces of baggage God never intended for you to carry. They'll weigh you down. And when crises come and you stumble, you'll fall hard. And all those pieces of luggage will come crashing down around you.

There are two things God doesn't want for you. First, *He never wants to cramp your style in life.* He wants you to live free and to enjoy Him and His world. But second, and more important, *God doesn't want you to hurt yourself.* The answer is to do what Paul in the Bible said to do and be very careful how you live:

- *Spend more hours in the safe zone.*
- *Watch your lifestyle.* If you've missed two or three days of devotions, Friday night is not the night to go out with friends who are going to make it tough for you to do the right thing.
- *Don't violate your conscience.* Maybe other people can have a beer and do intimate things

with their date and not get hurt. But if in your heart you know they're wrong for you, listen to your heart.

- *Do what God says for you to do.*
- *Be grown up and set an example.* Maybe there are things you can do that won't hurt you. But if by doing them, somebody else watching you might try them and get really bummed, back off. Set an example for your younger brother or sister who may be struggling with some things that might get them in trouble.

By spending more hours in the safe zone than in the grey zone and by asking God to help you do that, you'll find your life free from a lot of hassles and worries that are the results of bad decisions.

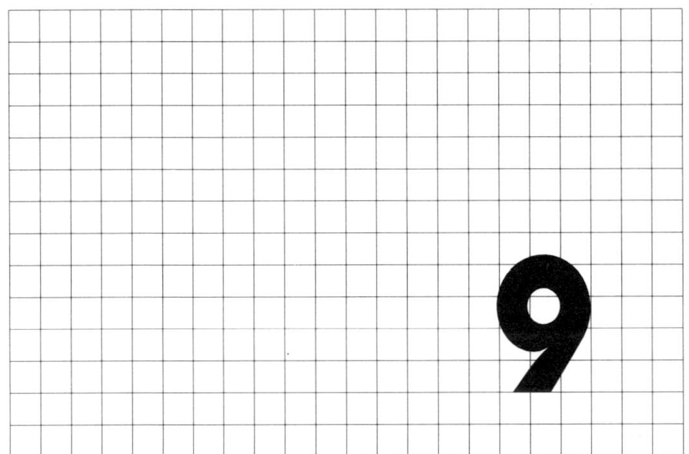

Some people call it "Sunday morning blues." Others call it "World War III." Whatever you call it, it comes out something like this: You want to sleep. God wants you to go to church. You want to go with friends to the beach. God wants you to go to church. The last thing you want is to spend an hour and a half of your time to go to a hot, stuffy building with a bunch of strangers. God wants you to go to church.

Everybody has a different opinion about going to church. Probably most of your friends don't even think twice about it. While you are headed to Sunday school and a morning of B-O-R-E-D-O-M, they're either sleeping in or headed out for a great day.

If people were normal at church you'd probably handle it better, but church always seems to attract people who you're glad are not your neighbors. Does it really matter to anyone, especially God, what you do with your Sunday? What in the world did God have in mind anyway, asking you to show up at this building every Sunday?

STARTING POINT 9

Going to church is part of God's good plan for your life.

Your bed probably feels better Sunday morning than any other morning of the week. That's the one morning you could sleep forever. But instead, that's the one morning out of all seven that God decided He wanted you in church. What did God have in mind, anyway?

Well, for one thing, God knew in advance that we would need times in our life to experience Him, to feel His power, and to hear His voice. You know the feeling. It comes when you're really down or super thankful. Maybe we don't walk around feeling like that every day, but now and then there are times when we need a visit with God.

When you became a Christian you joined a large family of people (some who have already died and others around the world) who also wanted to experience God. In hundreds of languages and in hundreds of thousands of places, Christians sense a need to take some time out of their busy days to thank God for what He has done for them. Setting aside some special time in the week for us to thank God for the good things that He has given us has been a part of God's plan since Day One.

Here are some good Bible verses that talk about church:

> Let us hold unswervingly to the hope we profess, for he who promised is faithful. And let us consider how we may spur one another on toward love and good deeds. Let us not give up meeting together, as some are in the habit of doing, but let us encourage one another—and all the more as you see the Day [of His coming back to earth] approaching.
>
> —HEBREWS 10:23–25 NIV

Church was designed by God to help you when things get tough. It's a place you can go to experience God and find the support you need from other Christians.

But some churches are more like corporations than families. That's too bad. God's idea was for your church to be alive and friendly. The church is meant to be a place for you to grow as a Christian, to learn how to make your life count.

A lot of teenagers (maybe even you) feel they experience God more in a Bible study or a walk in the woods at summer camp. You know, that's okay. In many ways you could call those activities church, because the Bible promises whenever two or three Christians get together, God will be right there with them helping them experience His presence.

There's no law that says church has to look a certain way or even be indoors. Church in a *building* is really our human interpretation of what we believe God wants from us in worshiping Him. It's steeped in thousands of years of tradition. Now, that doesn't make indoor church right or wrong, that just makes it the way we've been doing things for a few centuries.

What's most important to you is not where you *feel* church or what yours *looks* like. What's most important is *what can happen to you there.* Church can keep you on track. Your pastor or priest can give you helpful insights from the Bible on how to live and answer your big questions on God.

Church is also a place where you can meet people who think the same as you. Maybe you are not thinking about marriage yet, but dating the right kinds of people is important. You are more likely to find people who know God personally at church than you are likely to find them at any school party.

Going to church every Sunday isn't popular with a lot of Christians. Some Christians struggle to get up on a Sunday morning. Or Sunday seems like the best time to catch up on all the things you wanted to do last week. Maybe there are some other excuses—like it's too far to drive or your parents don't go each Sunday.

But hitting church every few weeks or even just once a week on Sunday is not God's idea of getting to know Him, worshiping Him, or being with other Christians. God is not looking for you to be uptight and in some kind of bondage to show up for church every Sunday.

God is looking for something else from you. He is looking for a commitment from you to get involved with Him in a good church, a place where the Bible is clearly explained and God is worshiped.

A study was conducted recently by a group of researchers. They found that societies that thrive over long periods of time have made religion the foundation of their lifestyle. Their finding supports what Christians already know: God knew what He was doing when He encouraged us in the Bible to worship Him regularly.

Let's put it this way: Not being involved in a church is missing God's best for your life. It's really not an option. And it takes commitment to go. Probably some of your Christian friends don't even feel that strongly about it. But if you want to experience God in your life and win over things that are tripping you up or if you want to meet some nice people worth dating, then get involved in church.

If you don't put this starting point in place, two things are going to happen to you. First, you won't be able to handle the temptations to do wrong and challenges that come along because you won't be getting fed the spiritual food you need. Sure, you can have your devotions every day and listen to

Christian music. But these don't give you enough support for your walk with God. You need the songs, the sermon, and especially the fellowship with other Christians to give you the boost you need to face life's challenges.

Second, your mind will start to play tricks on you. Maybe you've begun to feel like being a Christian isn't worth it, that "cool" people don't believe in the Lord. Going to church is one way to have a set of friends that will always care about you, who will help you think clearly about the important issues in your life.

But watch out! Going to church doesn't make you a Christian any more than singing along with Whitney Houston makes you a rock star. There's really no big payoff in just going. Some super religious people might get rude and put you on a guilt trip by saying, "You *have* to show up." But like we said before, God's not looking to tie you up in knots about this. He wants you to go faithfully because it's the one place during the week you can take time to experience Him along with other people.

Church is a place where you can be encouraged to hold on to the hope you found in God. It is a place where you can get to know the God who promised to be faithful to you no matter what happens to you or what you've done in life. It is a place where you can encourage other people—and other people can encourage you—to do good things.

Do you want to have spiritual power in your life and experience God? Then go where He is. **God is**

everywhere, but once a week in a special, unique way, you can go to a certain place and find God. Sure, there are a lot of decent and fun things to do on a Sunday morning like sleeping in, watching football, taking a trip, or just catching up on homework. But none of these things are going to give you the kind of strength and help you really want for the rest of your week. The only place you are going to find that is in church.

God never intended church to take the place of your talking to Him and reading His Word throughout the week. So if you try to make church the only time you get to know God each week, you're really going to be hurting. But God did want church to be a place where you can find other people who know Him and a place where you can take a break out of your life and find peace and quiet. Plus, going to church gives you an opportunity to thank Him for all of the good things He has done for you.

Check your attitude. Are you committed to going to church? Even if your parents don't go regularly? Even if all your friends think it's uncool? How about you? How strong is your commitment to meeting with God—at His house—each week?

Put this starting point in place in your life. Going to church is part of God's good plan for you.

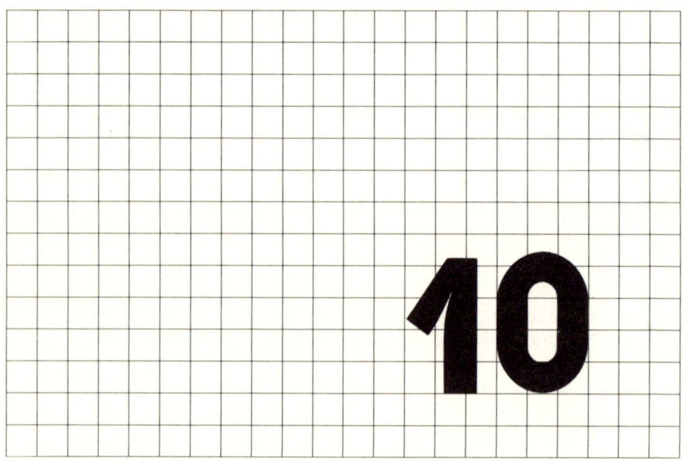

10

If any of your friends saw how long it took you to make up your mind what pair of pants to wear with what shirt just to go out Friday night to the movies, they'd say you had totally lost it.

Your friends primp, too, and work just as hard as you do to be cool when they show up. That's just part of living. We like to make sure people see us and don't forget us.

Take this test: *What did that certain, special person you happen to like have on today?* You probably could describe him or her right down to the shoelaces. See? When something matters to you, it makes an impression on you. Leaving impressions and being impressed are just a part of living. And that takes us to our next starting point.

STARTING POINT 10

Live life at the right temperature.

You've probably heard people talk about someone living life "too fast," or going through life "too slow." In fact, you probably know people who move too fast (like last Friday night's date) or people who move too slow (like the guy you wish would get off his duff and call you for a date). Everybody lives life at a certain speed, and in fact, a certain temperature.

Did you ever stop to think about that one? What temperature you live your life is as important as how fast you live it. Let's say you should live life at just the right temperature—not too hot and not too cold. Would you know the best temperature for your life?

Well, God has an idea on this. In fact, **God made the whole world to function at certain temperatures.** If the temperature of the sun were to increase by just one degree, ice would melt, oceans would rise, and whole cities like Miami and Los Angeles would be wiped out. God's got His hand on the great temperature gauge in nature so the whole universe will function at certain temperatures, even in the sub-zero cold of outer space.

In the same way, God knows the right tem-

perature for your life. You know what it is? It's the temperature that allows good impressions to be left on you and bad ones to roll off you. If you live life too hot, too fast, certain basic things are going to happen. You're going to miss things, things that are really important. You'll miss a hurting friend who needs a helping hand from you. You'll miss your grandmother who needs a letter or a visit from you. You'll miss important times with your family and friends. You'll miss these things because you'll be running around too fast looking for the next high. You'll offend people, too, because there's just no time to have good manners or be kind. You'll cut people off while you're driving because you try to do too much before school and end up being late for first period.

When you're living too hot in life, you're just thinking of yourself. And that stinks on ice. Something else. When you run too hot in life, nothing sticks. You're like hot wax in the top of a candle—every time you try to make an impression in it, the heat from the candle melts the mark away.

Like we said before, **God has a blueprint for your life. Like a house builder, He's eager to build something beautiful and worthwhile.** To do that, God allows good and bad things to happen in your life. God allows all these lasting, permanent impressions to be made in order to show that things go best when He's in control. God never permits things to happen without regard for what's best for you. Sometimes people mistake pain in their life as God acting tough. That's just not true. God allows these things so you'll live life at the right temperature. He does it through circumstances, the Bible, and other people. But if you run too hot, the good impressions God tries to leave in your life will be eradicated, just like the hot wax impressions in the top of a candle will melt into nothing. You miss out on God's best for you by overheating.

A similar thing can happen if you run too cold. Do you know what happens when you live life too cold? You become brittle. (Ever drop an ice cube? It cracks and breaks.) Your feelings get hurt too easily by things people say. If somebody doesn't invite you to a party, you get depressed for three days. If you don't feel accepted by your friends because of your weight, you start binging and purging. Instead of being like hot wax, you're like cold wax. You get so set in your ways and brittle that few impressions are left on you at all. God tries to impress something good on you, but you're just too hardened for Him to get through.

What's the solution to all this? Your starting point has to be to live life at the right temperature. And the right temperature is not hard to find at all. Here's how: Make a commitment to be a pliable person. "Yet, O LORD, you are our Father. We are the clay, you are the potter; we are all the work of your hand" (Isaiah 64:8 NIV).

One of our starting points at the beginning of this book was, "Like it or not, God is in charge." When you came to know God personally, you turned your life (a big lump of clay) over to God. In one sense you said to Him, "God take this lump of clay and make something of it. I can't do it on my own." That's what it means to turn your life over to God. God is like this Great Pottery Maker, and He takes the lump of clay of your life and He makes impressions on it. But if your life is too cold, or too hot, those impressions won't stick. He made you to be pliable. He put just enough ingredients in the clay of your life so that you could be pliable with His help. You can ask God to help you do this: "Teach us to number our days and recognize how few they are; help us to spend them as we should" (Psalm 90:12 NIV). King David asked God for help in this, too.

When David said, "Lord, teach us to number our days," he meant "God help us not to waste our lives. Help us to recognize how few days there really are in life." It's hard to believe when you're a teenager there's anything going on past next weekend. But there is. Ask any adult, and you'll be told just how short life is. Recognizing how few days there are will help you live life at the right temperature.

Some final thoughts: Some people think God wants us to live a cold, boring life. Lots of kids rebel against that and end up living life too hot. They miss out on experiencing the pleasure of helping others, waiting for sex in marriage, or learning an important lesson. They live life at the wrong temperature.

The Bible says God gave us everything in life to enjoy. It all comes down to handling your life the right way and living it at the right temperature. This is an important starting point. Put it in place in your life. Understand that God brings impressions along to help you live. Accept everything that comes at you. Make each day count, and you'll find living life at just the right temperature is the only way to go.

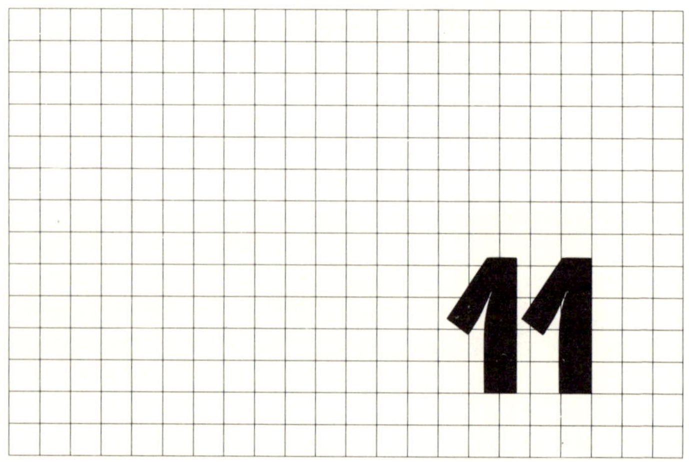

She was one of the healthiest kids at the beach that summer. Her arms and legs were as strong and pretty as any teenage girl could ever want. She could hold her own against many guys when it came to swimming. She was happy. She came from a good home with sufficient money. She had a bright future in a college somewhere.

But it all changed in a split second one afternoon with a dive into the bay. She went into the water healthy with everything going for her. But Joni Eareckson Tada came out of the water paralyzed and her life changed forever.

And then there was Dave Roever. Dave was your basic, average teenager who felt serving his country made good sense. So off to the Vietnam War he went, hating the war, but feeling that if he could give Communism one more slap in the face, then somehow it would be worth it. But one day on river patrol, his boat was ambushed and a sniper's bullet blew up an incendiary grenade in his hand, mutilating his upper torso, hands, and most of all, his face.

Joni and Dave, two teenagers just like you, had everything going for them. They had a little money in their pockets. Parents who loved them. Bright, happy futures. But each of them faced a day when life went crazy and they had to redefine what living was all about.

They had to redefine what it meant to be happy and comfortable in life. Most people who looked at them said their lives were over, they couldn't be happy anymore.

But it wasn't that way at all. Both found a way to rise above their lousy circumstances and find meaning and happiness in life.

What you can learn from Joni and Dave is different from what most of your friends are saying. TV screams it at you, and so does radio, your friends, and billboards: Trying to be happy is a worthwhile pursuit in life. In fact, being happy is the way life is supposed to be lived. You're supposed to have a super-cushy life, and your comfort is your due.

What does God say about this? Is this the way you are supposed to live? What happens when life falls apart?

If your number one pursuit in life is to be comfortable and hang out with beautiful people, you're going to miss God's best for your life by a country mile. (And that's a long ways! A *country mile* is "the distance between your seat in homeroom and the seat of somebody you happen to like a lot.")

Hey, let's talk turkey for a minute. The Bible says God is love, right? Right. And when you love somebody you take care of that person, right? Right. So that means that if God loves you He'll take care of you, give you everything you need, and basically let you do whatever you want as long as you keep your nose clean, right? Wrong.

Wrong? That's right. Wrong, because it's a myth that God wants you to be a healthy, wealthy, happily married, beautiful, well-educated, popular, successful person. Ask Joni or Dave.

The myth makes sense until you dive in a bay one day and come up crippled or a grenade goes off and blows half your face away. Or unless you were born with a disability or a defect. Then you begin to wonder why God, the Big Candy Man, didn't deliver for you. You get hurt and disillusioned with how God treated you.

And that's part of the problem. While God wants you to experience life in all its fullness, His ideas on how that should happen don't always include being comfortable.

Life at His best for you may mean there's some pain involved. God can allow you to be healthy, wealthy, beautiful, and popular—but He doesn't have to, and sometimes He simply won't.

Oftentimes, God does give you a good thing. He'll give you a good job, a special friend, or some extra money. But what God chooses to bless you with is based on His choice, not on anything you can do to earn it.

Not picking up a *Playboy* for a month doesn't suddenly earn you a date with the prettiest girl in school. Or not talking bad about somebody for a week or two doesn't suddenly earn you the World's Greatest Christian Award.

That's bad math, because your good works and special blessings are not an equation. God makes up His own mind about what He will allow in your life, both good and bad.

Since God allows and chooses certain things for you, you need to know that every one of His choices—those that look like gifts and those that look like booby prizes—are based on love. They are based on what is best for you.

It's easy to say the following are best for you: good healthy body, nice looks, dates with a steady friend, a good job, extra bucks in your pocket, nice clothes, a nice home, a new car, and perpetual happiness.

But what's best for you in life is not always what's easiest. Now look at this list. Would you say these would be best for you? A lost job, feelings of depression, rejection by a certain college, a wrecked car, a broken back, a retarded brother, divorced parents, a flunked test, a breakup with somebody you really care about, school friends who get down on you, or betrayal by your best friend.

For sure, none of those things look like they're best for you. *But God can use bad things for good in your life.* (No, they don't *feel* good. And anyone who says you should act like they don't bother you is your basic jerk. God never intended for you to feel pain and then pretend that it didn't bother you. You've got to be a real person, even when it hurts.)

STARTING POINT 11

God is more interested in you becoming a whole person than He is in you being comfortable.

The decision to follow Christ is a tough one. Christ doesn't promise you an easy life, but He does promise you a whole life. One full of good things. In fact, once when Jesus was talking He said, "I have come that they [you] may have life, and have it more abundantly" (John 10:10 NKJV).

Do you know what that word *abundant* means? It means "all your needs are supplied." That is God's idea for what is important for you in life—a life with all of your *needs* met, not a life of cushy comfort with all your *wants* met. That doesn't mean God won't give you things you want. It does mean His first priority and commitment is to give you things you need. God will give you what you want if you ask Him for it and if it's according to His good plan for your life.

There are some great verses in the Bible that can help you get your priorities straight. They are found in two different letters that Paul wrote. One was to his young friend Timothy:

> But godliness with contentment is great gain. For we brought nothing into the world, and we can take nothing out of it. But if we have food and clothing, we will be content with that. People who want to get rich fall into temptation and a trap and into many foolish and harmful desires that plunge men into ruin and destruction. For the love of money is a root of all kinds of evil. Some people, eager for money, have wandered from the faith and pierced themselves with many griefs.
>
> —1 TIMOTHY 6–10 NIV

The second was to his friends in Rome:

> We can rejoice, too, when we run into problems and trials for we know that they are good for us— they help us learn to be patient. And patience develops strength of character in us and helps us trust God more each time we use it until finally our hope and faith are strong and steady.
>
> —ROMANS 5:3–4 TLB

These verses say problems are good for us—they help us grow up. They also say we have to learn to live a life that pleases God. That is what godliness means. Nothing more than that. Godliness is not some pie-in-the-sky, super-religious kind of thing. Godliness is simply living a life that pleases God and accepting your circumstances.

As a young Christian, you will have to separate yourself from the way some Christians think and from the way the world thinks when it comes to comfort.

Right in your own church, dozens of people believe it's okay to buy the biggest house they can afford, join the most important country club, and send their kids to the best colleges. But just because some Christians act that way doesn't make it right for you. You've got to go back to God's Word. God says living a life that pleases Him and learning to be content and independent of your changeable circumstances is great gain.

God's idea of great gain is a sense of joy, similar to what clothes, a job, or success might bring you only deeper, better, and longer.

Believe it or not, hundreds of kids in your high school walk around feeling empty inside. They spend their nights crying themselves to sleep asking the question, *Why am I so empty?* Oftentimes, those same kids, some of them your friends, turn to drugs or even suicide. But they don't find any answers there. Jesus, the one who promised to give them life and to give it to them abundantly, is the answer.

It's possible to be a Christian, to devote yourself to being comfortable and wealthy, and to end up just as empty. It can happen if you never find out what it means to live a contented life that pleases God.

Ask God to help you put this starting point to work in your life. Accept the fact that God is more interested in your wholeness than He is in your comfort. He allows hurt and pain into your life to build fiber and maturity in you, to sandpaper the rough edges in your life, to make you a better and stronger person. He wants you to be someone He can count on to share the Good News of Christ with others. The sandpapering of those rough spots will help toughen you to life's punches, teach you what really counts in life, and force you to go back to God—and that's always good for us, no matter what makes it happen.

There are twists and turns on the road of life. But God promised to be there with you every step of the way. Every time you sink into a pothole or make a bad turn, God will be there to lend a helping hand. Don't get suckered into believing that trouble in your life is God getting even with you because of some attitude you had or something you did wrong.

It's hard to believe when you live in North America that God doesn't want you to be happy, comfortable, and have money. But if you got on a plane and flew around the world, you'd soon see that being rich and comfortable is *not* the way the whole world lives.

Three-fourths of the world doesn't have a clue as to how good it really is here in the United States.

The poorest people in our country would be considered well off to them. And in those countries, you'll find millions of Christians who have come to know and experience God's goodness—and they aren't nearly so comfortable and wealthy as even you are. Knowing this should make you think differently about how concerned God really is with your comfort.

God's plan for Joni and Dave was that through some pain in their lives they would become whole people and would become all He wanted them to be.

God's best for you might include some pain and some hurt. But remember: *The pain God allows comes from His loving hand.* He won't allow anything to happen to you that will hurt you beyond what you can take. God loves you; His plans are good for you; His plans bring hope to your life. That's what the Bible means when it says God is good.

Put this important starting point in your life and you'll find more and more freedom to accept whatever comes along in your life.

Don't you hate it when your parents give you a hassle about your room?

They say, "How can you live like that?"

"It's easy, Mom. You should try it," you reply.

Unimpressed, your mother says, "Make your bed and put your clothes away before you leave."

"I just hung them there on the chair an hour ago."

"Your room is out of control. You better get on with putting it back in order," your mother orders.

"Out of control? I just cleaned it up two weeks ago!"

Parents can really get bent out of shape about things like your room, coming in on time, or parking the car a certain way in the driveway, can't they? They seem to like things under control. Do your parents know something you don't? Let's find out.

Every day you live, you've got choices to make—whether to speak to somebody who is weird, whether to do your chores and your homework, whether to work on a research paper. People everywhere struggle with making good choices about doing things they ought to do at the right time. In fact, there are dozens of books on time management that teach people in business how to do things they ought to do at the right time. People everywhere are trying to get control of their time and their life and their money.

That's because what they know they should do and what they feel like doing don't always fit. It's like a war sometimes to do the right thing at the right time and to have self-control. Other times you just sort of slip into something without really being careful. As a Christian, God is very concerned that you accomplish what He has planned for you.

To be a winner in life, you've got to have self-control.

Self-control is an ugly word today. A lot of people don't like to talk about self-control. It sounds like work, doesn't it? Like a lot of pain and hassle. Like you've got to give up a lot of things you really enjoy.

The problem is, if you don't have self-control you get sloppy. And you end up bouncing off walls because you do only the things you feel like doing. People who lack self-control end up being video freaks or becoming computer nuts. They end up watching too much TV or becoming overweight. People who lack self-control are always mouthing off with something smart to say to everybody. They just never learned to control how they talk.

Usually people who lack self-control are not the most fun people to be with. On the other hand, people who are balanced and who learn to do the right things at the right time often are really "together" people who accomplish a lot in life.

If you play in the band or orchestra, you know it takes self-control to say no to other interests and go practice. It takes self-control to refuse dessert if you have trouble with being overweight. It takes self-control to run an extra set of 880's when you know you need the extra practice.

But that's the winning edge God intends for you to have in life. Self-control. How do you go about getting it?

Almost everyone is not good at having it. In fact, that's why all those self-help books are written. Everyone seems to need a little help.

God put some good thoughts in the Bible about what self-control will do for you.

> And to knowledge, add self-control; and to self-control, perseverance; and to perseverance, godliness; and to godliness, brotherly kindness; and to brotherly kindness, love. For if you possess these qualities in increasing measure, they will keep you from being ineffective and unproductive in your knowledge of our Lord Jesus Christ. But if anyone does not have them, he is nearsighted and blind, and has forgotten that he has been cleansed from his past sins.
>
> —2 PETER 1:6–9 NIV

The Bible says self-control is something you need to add to your life; it is not something you are born with. But when you do add it, you'll grow stronger spiritually and become more fruitful and more useful to God.

Do you ever get frustrated with yourself spiritually? Maybe you struggle with sex. You've been having sex and you know you shouldn't. Or maybe you're having solo sex and you feel guilty. You've tried to stop but just can't. Maybe you've never been able to keep your room clean for more than two hours straight. Or you're overweight, can't seem to study enough, or you say mean things sometimes.

Self-control can help you in these areas. God wants to help you with every one of these things so you're in control and not out of control. Sometimes it's frustrating to read the Bible's warnings about having control over your passions and body. The Bible never seems to tell you how to do it. And when you've been struggling with something like solo sex (or anything else you don't seem to have victory over in your life), it's tough to know how to have self-control.

But that's where those verses in the Bible *can* help you. Remember what it said? "And to knowledge, add self-control; and to self-control, perseverance." That's the key right there. If you are going to have self-control in life, you've got to first know what's right and wrong. That takes knowing the Bible. Somehow, just knowing what's right and wrong helps you at least know what the options are.

Is something troubling you in life that you have never been able to win over? Ask God to show you what He wants. He'll show you what's right and wrong. That's really half of the battle, just knowing what you should do. The second half of the battle is doing what you know you should do. That's the tougher part. But look what the Bible says to do. It says once you know what's right and wrong, be self-controlled. And to be self-controlled, you have to add perseverance to your life.

Perseverance is something anyone can learn. It means taking small steps, one at a time. It's a little bit like running a cross-country race. The way to win is to gut it out. Put one foot in front of the other. Persevere.

God knows that self-control doesn't come easy. But He also knows that if we persevere in life, we learn to have self-control. That's why God put things in that order in the Bible. And that's what self-control and self-discipline are. It is remembering what's important and then doing it one step at a time.

Self-control means you do your chores first, like cutting the grass, and then split to go have fun with your friends. You know something? Being self-controlled is more important than being clever and cute. It's not something you can take a course in, but it is something that shows in how you live. It touches on little things like making your bed, doing your chores, spending time reading the Bible, doing your homework on time, not speeding, or not going too far with your date.

Sometimes having self-control means doing all the stuff you don't like to do. But look, there are big payoffs when you do it.

By putting this starting point in place in your life, the Bible says you are going to learn to grow strong spiritually. Sometimes those big struggles you have with sex and doing the right thing wear you out. They make you feel down. But when you know what is right and wrong and you persevere, you'll grow strong spiritually. And those struggles will become smaller and smaller. Doing the right thing will become more and more natural. And it's not going to wear you out. You're going to be up more and feel great knowing you're doing things God's way. And that is what God's plan has been for you all along.

But it doesn't come easy. Of all the things you face, self-control is one of the toughest battles. You don't learn it in a year. It might take you five or ten years to learn to be self-controlled in every area of your life. But the time to get started is right now.

Put this starting point in place in your life. Remember, learn what's important, then go and do it a step at a time. In little ways (like getting your parents off your back about your room) it will be great! But in big ways it will help you make good decisions and stick to doing the right thing. In the end, you are going to respect yourself more and get more out of life.

On Monday, everyone you sit with at lunch has the clearest complexion and face imaginable. Not one person has zits. In Tuesday's gym class, it's thin city except for you and two other people. Wednesday rolls around and you get your chemistry test back. Great, only three people did better than you, but you still weren't the best in the class. Thursday—the last day you can expect to get a date—your best friend got one, but for you no dice. Friday, your older sister throws a party. Twelve people come over and you couldn't even get one other person to go shopping with you. Saturday you make $25 doing fries at McDonald's all day; your sister makes $35 selling jewelry door to door. Finally it's Sunday, and you sit down in youth group and look around. Every person there, you know, is more spiritual than you.

Seven days a week, seven people or seven thousand. Every person in your life means a new standard you have to meet. From school to church, there's always someone out there who is better than you. It makes you wonder sometimes what you're worth anyway, doesn't it?

Do you ever wonder what good you are to the world anyway? It always seems that someone else is better than you at everything. Someone else can always run faster, do better in chemistry, have more friends, or come from a better family. When you're faced with a lot of sharp people, sometimes it's hard to believe in yourself. That's why this starting point is so important:

STARTING POINT 13

Believe in yourself the same way God believes in you.

One of the original rock 'n' roll singers sang a song that said, "I'm all I've got." That singer was believing in herself. And that's a very important thing for you to do in life, too.

Believing in yourself means that you respect and take care of yourself because you know how valuable you are to God and to others. But how do you get there? How do you ever get to a point where you really believe in yourself the way you want to? Believing in yourself means that you have to balance two voices, two ideas, inside of you. One voice says, *Hey, scumbag, you're a worm.* Another voice says, *Hey, you're so worthy, don't ask God for a Cadillac; expect one and tell Him what color you want.* Everyone hears both: "You're a scumbag" and "You're worth a million dollars." How you react to opposing voices will make a difference in your life.

Sometimes we set our standards too high. We think no one ever ate alone in the cafeteria and survived, flunked a test and got into college, dropped a tray and had any friends after that, or wrecked the car **and lived to tell about it.** When some very normal things happen to us which aren't pleasant, we feel down and life looks really rotten. That's when trouble hits. Our eating and dress habits, our morals, and our attitude can go basically right down the tubes. Why? Because we didn't see ourselves the way God sees us.

The Bible has some very good ideas for you about how valuable you are to this world, the people around you, and yourself.

Several thousand years ago, God told one of the people who wrote the Bible to write this down: "I have loved you with an everlasting love" (Jeremiah 31:3 NIV). Check that out—*everlasting.* That means "forever," "no changes." *Nothing you have ever done or ever will do can change the fact that God loves you.* God will always act with love toward you. Always. When God said He'll *love* you, He promised an ongoing action. God's love means that He'll be faithful to you, He'll never lie to you. He'll always give you what is best for you. He'll guide you and guard you from trouble. And He'll always forgive you, even when you make mistakes.

You need to let it sink into your brain that the God of the universe, who simply spoke things into existence, cares so much about you that He promised to love you forever. There is another place in the Bible that describes God's love for you. A writer by the name of Paul said:

> For I am convinced that nothing can ever separate us from his love. Death can't, and life can't. The angels won't, and all the powers of hell itself cannot keep God's love away. Our fears for today, our worries about tomorrow, or where we are—high above the sky, or in the deepest ocean—nothing will ever be able to separate us from the love of God demonstrated by our Lord Jesus Christ when he died for us.
>
> —ROMANS 8:38–39 TLB

The best demonstration that God loves you and that you are valuable is the fact that He sent Christ to earth to reconcile you back to Himself. God didn't do that for giraffes or tulips or the rocks on the mountains, but He did it for you. You aren't junk; God doesn't make junk.

Right about now maybe you're saying, "Big deal. So God loves me. What does that have to do with believing in myself?"

If God is willing to do all of these things to show His love for you, that means you have value to Him and to people around you. Oh, you may not feel it (back to the starting point about faith—remember that one? learning to balance faith with feelings?), but that doesn't change anything.

Just as God's love for you is an action word, you've got to have some action in your own life if you are going to believe yourself the right way. You've got to find the balance between thinking you're a scumbag and you're worth a million dollars. You are going to need God's help. He'll give it.

Ask God to help you. He'll plant the seeds for believing in yourself if you ask Him. Build your skills. Learn to do things. Find out what you're good at and then build on it. If you are a musician, practice the piano more. Take up a hobby. Look for good in people. Observe good manners when you meet people. In every job you do, do it well. Dress well. Eat well. Take care of your body, mind, and soul. Stay away from things like drugs and beer that tear you down. Don't let things happen to you that will hurt you.

God needs "together" people. That's a good reason to believe in yourself. God needs people who are balanced in what they think of themselves in this world. A "together you" is His best way of letting others know who He *is*.

Here's something to remember: *The biggest thing in life isn't getting a date for Homecoming. You will survive.* So many people get bummed out when they don't get to go to certain parties. What you do with your life is far more important.

If you believe in yourself (as God does), you're going to be able to do some things in life that count. You sometimes probably feel like saying, "What's the use? I can't make any difference in this world." Maybe you feel that taxes can't solve poverty or that we are all going to blow up in a nuclear war, so why even vote? But the fact is, God put gifts and talents and abilities in you that are extremely valuable.

If you believe in yourself (as God does), you'll find that you have confidence to do an awful lot of things that you once thought wouldn't count. You'll be able to make important decisions better because you'll have confidence that you can handle it.

Do you know some people have sex with other people because they do not like themselves? They do things like having sex or getting high because they are struggling to find out who they are and what their real value is. Maybe you have a friend who dresses punk or you know someone who has an eating disorder. Maybe that describes you. **When you accept who you are and how valuable you are to God and to others, you'll find you don't have to dress a certain way or be super thin to be loved and accepted.** Your friends will enjoy you just the way you are. And let's face it, sometimes guys drive bad, too fast in dangerous places because they don't really know who they are. They're trying to impress themselves and their friends. But when you know what your real value is before God, you're at peace with yourself and you don't have to show off to feel good.

But you've got to watch out. On TV you might hear someone say, "Hey, respect yourself. You're not bad, just do what you want to do because you're worth it." The hassle with this is, what people are really telling you is to be selfish, take care of yourself first, make yourself comfortable, and take what you deserve. But this isn't the real path to believing in yourself. You've got to start with the right idea. *The right idea is that you are worth something because of how God made you and what He has done for you.*

Do you realize it is wrong to not love what God loves? If you believe in yourself, you are going to respect yourself. You are going to find that you are trustworthy, that you can give and receive love, and that you can be proud in the right way of your accomplishments in life. You'll be grateful for things that happen to you. You won't have to show off and be cool. You won't have to have sex, be thin, or dress a certain way to be accepted.

Are you looking for a new start in life? Maybe you get mad easily or you're bitter about something. Maybe you've been really super temperamental because you haven't been believing in yourself. Hey, believe in yourself.

Do you want to know how to do that? The Bible tells you how: "Let everyone be sure that he is doing his very best, for then he will have the personal satisfaction of work well done, and won't need to compare himself with someone else" (Galatians 6:4 TLB).

There's the key. Do your best in life with whatever you've got. Give it your best. Set high standards for yourself. Even though you may not meet them, do your best. Then you're going to be satisfied with what you've done and you won't need to compare yourself with someone else. That's good practical advice, and it comes from God.

Accept yourself for who you are. Don't try to be something you are not. Just work hard and accept the fact that God loves you and always will love you. By believing in yourself this way, you'll find that you can achieve things in life you never thought possible.

You have taken a different route to class so you can meet a certain person. You have slowed down so that your paths will cross. All of a sudden it happens. Your plan is working, and that certain person is coming right at you. Your heart races and you manage to squeak out this little, "Hi, how are you?" Perfect timing! Now, if you can just go out together. . . .

Nobody has to tell you how important timing is in life. It takes some serious planning to cross paths with someone you like. Asking for (and getting) the car for Saturday night takes some pretty careful timing somewhere back around Wednesday. And what about sports like football? Move a half-second too early, and you earn your team an offside penalty and yourself a seat on the bench.

Good timing is important in a lot of things in life—sports, music, dates, you name it. To have good timing in life, you have to keep your eye on the clock. The right clock. There are basically two clocks in life, the clock everyone watches and the clock God watches. It's easy to live every day with our clock because we develop our own sense of timing about things. But God has a clock, too, and that's why this starting point is so extremely important.

STARTING POINT 14

Develop God's sense of timing in your life.

Most of us never really think about God's clock, but it's real. It's some kind of mongo, super-quartz clock that's always accurate, never misses a beat. The clock God uses sometimes tells a time different from ours. That's why it's important to develop His sense of timing. After all, God has everything in His control, right down to some of the smallest details about your life. If He is helping to arrange what happens in your life, it makes a lot of sense to understand His sense of timing.

One way God's sense of timing is different from yours is that God sees your life more as a process than as a series of big events. Sometimes we get into the habit of moving from one big event to another, from a party, to a vacation, to a big date, to a football game. In fact, we get moving so fast sometimes, moving from one big event to another, that we don't even eat right. You know, instant lunch and supper popped right from the microwave, or a quick, fast-food hamburger and fries. It seems that people are in too much of a hurry to eat right because they're off to the next big happening. **Seems like everybody is always going for the big event, the Super Bowl of Something. It starts to make you feel like life is one big event after another.**

Now don't freak out. Big events in life like Amy Grant concerts, the Super Bowl, the prom, or the Olympics make life better. They give you something to look forward to. But is living for them realistic? Can you ever get too much of a good thing? What happens if your team doesn't make it to the Super Bowl or you don't get accepted into a certain club?

When life becomes all big events, we miss opportunities to enjoy simple things, like doing something kind for someone else or just enjoying nature. We get all hung up on being entertained, and then we start to look for highs to keep us high. We get down between big events waiting for the next big deal. We get impatient when life gets a little boring. So we push our boundaries a little. Maybe we go a little further than we should with someone we care about or try drinking some Friday night at a friend's house. We end up compromising when we begin looking for what feels good.

If life was all just feeling good and big events, this might not be a problem, but sometimes big events are bad—you lose one of your parents, you get seriously sick, or you don't get accepted to a certain school. Or how about this: What if all your life you were taught that sex before marriage was wrong, and then one night you went the whole way with your date? You would feel like your entire life was ruined by that one big event. (Even though you'd have to pay the consequences for it, God promises to forgive you when you make a mistake this big.)

When we think life is just one big event after another and something bad happens to us, it can blow us away, make us feel like failures. Some teenagers even end up killing themselves because life got messed up and they felt they couldn't ever recover from a bad, big event in their life.

Somehow, we've got to look at life differently, not as all big events to entertain us or just bad, big events to blow us away. We need to see things as God sees them. For God, there's really only one truly big event in your life that's important—that's the day you came to know Him personally and to believe in Jesus Christ as the answer to your life's problems. God spends a lot of time making sure you come to know Him, arranging all the events just right so that you hear about Him.

That doesn't mean He doesn't care about the rest

of your life, however. In fact, the Bible says God cares a lot about your everyday decisions, and that's why he gives you guidance through your prayers and your Bible. But in God's point of view, there's only one really big event. The rest of the time, God sees the world differently. He sees the world in process. He sees that He started the world someplace and that it will end someplace. He was there at the beginning and He'll be there at the end. That's important to you, because that means we're going somewhere.

Do you ever feel lost in life? Like you don't know what to do next? Like you wonder if you can make something out of your life with the grades you've got? God sees the beginning and the end of your life. He knows the day you were born and knows the day you will die. While He's concerned about all the events in your life, He's not focused on them. God sees the big picture, and He invites you to do the same thing. Once Peter wrote a letter to some friends and told them, "Cast all your anxiety upon him [Jesus] because he cares for you" (1 Peter 5:7 NIV). That means that what happens in your life, God can help you handle. And you don't have to worry about what's ahead or what's behind. That's a part of developing God's sense of timing in your life, too—not worrying about the past or the future, but just going God's speed a day at a time.

Because you can't live or love in the past or the future, it's better to go at God's pace, at just the right timing that He has for your life. Living in today's world and not next weekend is really important to you. In our country, a lot of people tend to work five days a week to finance everything they do on their weekends—renting videos, going shopping, or just having fun. God's not against any of those things. But he never intended us to work five days a week to finance two days of fun on the weekend. He never intended that we should live from one weekend to the next. He never wanted us to spend five days working just to provide ourselves with a cushy living the two days we're off on the weekend.

God has a better idea. His plan is that we live each day to the fullest, doing what we can to help others, and using our talents to make something meaningful of our life on Tuesday, as well as Saturday.

One man wrote thousands of years ago about God's sense of timing. His name was Solomon, and he was one of the wisest men who ever lived. Here's what he wrote:

> Everything is appropriate in its own time. But though God has planted eternity in the hearts of men, even so, many cannot see the whole scope of God's work from beginning to end. So I conclude that, first, there is nothing better for a man than to be happy and to enjoy himself as long as he can; and second, that he should eat and drink and enjoy the fruits of his labors, for these are gifts from God. And I know this, that whatever God does is

final—nothing can be added or taken from it; God's purpose in this is that man should fear the all-powerful God.

—ECCLESIASTES 3:11–14 TLB

Do you see what Solomon said? He said that everything works together. Everything has its own appropriate time. When you walk with God, everything in your life is moving towards some important end.

Maybe in church, sometimes, you've heard people talk about how they met that certain person at a strategic time in their life. There are thousands and thousands of times throughout history when God planned strategic meetings. He allowed things to happen that brought certain people together in a certain way. That's how God works. That's what the Bible means when it says, "Everything is appropriate in its own time."

God does this because He wants you to respect Him and honor Him and trust His sense of timing in your life, especially when things don't work out right and you get disappointed because you feel you got left behind, or left out. But remember this: *Everything in the whole universe is under God's control.* Everything in your life is under His control when you pray and talk with Him about your life.

God still plans strategic meetings, even in today's world. He'll plan them for you, too, if you have enough faith to believe He can do that for you. But to get in on some of these strategic meetings, you've got to be on time. And to be on time, you've got to know when to show. And to know when to show, you've got to know the one who keeps the clock, and that's God. Want to get to know God? Read His Word.

All throughout the Bible, you'll see different timing commands God gives us. Check these out:

- "**Stop** listening to teaching that contradicts what you know is right" (Proverbs 19:27 TLB).
- "**Go** and make disciples in all the nations" (Matthew 28:19 TLB).
- "He who is **slow** to wrath has great understanding" (Proverbs 14:29 NKJV).
- "Rest in the Lord; **wait** patiently for him to act" (Psalm 37:7 TLB).

Stop. Go. Slow down. Wait. The whole universe, including your life, runs on those commands God gives. All those strategic meetings you hear about or long for in your life can happen. There's nothing random in this universe. Everything we see in the heavens, in our life, is there by design. The universe, our earth, who you meet and when you meet, all come about *at just the right time* for two reasons—so we will honor and respect God for (1) who He is and for (2) His ability to control the universe's great clock.

Those little commands of the clock are important to you. God has you slow down in life, speed up, wait, go forward, or stop so that you'll miss trouble and won't get hit hard in life. When God says to stop doing something, He's telling you to stop for your own good. When He says, "Go forward," He's telling you to go forward so that you'll see something. When He says, "Slow down" or "Speed up" or "Wait," God's really saying, "Be careful, I want you to arrive on time where I've got you going."

Sometimes it's hard to imagine God's sense of timing is for our good. We have car accidents, fail tests, or don't get to meet people we want to meet. But remember, we talked about this earlier. God is a God of love. Everything He does in your life, He does for a reason, for your own good so that you'll grow and become a strong person.

Developing God's sense of timing in your life is very important. It will help you quit seeing your whole life as one big event that, if blown, will ruin your life forever. Knowing God's sense of timing will help you quit wasting your life by running from one big Super Bowl to the next. Knowing God's sense of timing in your life will help you realize that every day counts, that you should make the most of every day, and quit living five days just to get to the weekend to party. And one more thing, knowing God's sense of timing in your life will help you show up at just the right time at some pretty strategic meetings.

There are things for you to do in this world, things to help others, things to do for yourself. There are people you need to meet, people who will brighten and change your life, people who need what you have to offer. But for you to get in on those strategic meetings, you have to know God's sense of timing—and you get that from talking with Him every day and reading the Bible.

God's sense of timing is more living day-to-day than it is living big-event-to-big-event. Ask God to give you His sense of timing, and you'll find that you'll be showing up for some really exciting meetings!

15

*You can hardly go to a PG-rated movie
these days without hearing it. You hear
it in the locker room when a locker door
gets slammed on somebody's finger. You
hear it after an algebra test and in the
cafeteria. You hear it in a lot of places. If
people don't get what they want, they get
hurt or angry—and out comes some very
"religious" talk. Yep, it's religious talk
alright, but not the way you're accus-
tomed to hearing the name of the Lord
used.*

If you're a sensitive person and you hear
someone use the name of God in a swearing way, it hurts your ears. And somewhere deep
inside, you know it's not right. It's not right because
the third commandment said it's not right.

When somebody swears like that, what do you

do? Usually there are two voices inside, aren't there? One says, *Speak up. Say to the person, "Hey, watch your language."* But a second voice says, *Hey, don't wear your Christianity like a big headband or a badge.* Usually the one voice ends up being a little louder than the other, and you just bite your tongue and walk away.

Is that the right response? Or are you supposed to go through life telling people who talk different from you to cool off? That sounds like an intrusion on somebody's rights, doesn't it? On the other hand, are you supposed to go through life as a Christian never standing up for Christ? What's the real right answer here?

Swearing is a pretty small thing. But some day down the road, you may be asked to stand up for your faith in Jesus Christ—and your life may depend on it. You may be asked to make some moral choices (perhaps to marry a person who doesn't know God or to do something in a job that's dishonest), and right at that moment you're going to be asked to stand up for Christ. And those two voices are going to speak to you. One will say, *Speak up.* The other will say, *Don't wear your Christianity like a badge.* What will you do?

STARTING POINT 15

Have courage to speak up for Christ.

Most of us don't really like the idea of speaking up for Christ. Our American way of living is really quite private. (Time out for a 30-second history lesson: If you went clear back to the beginning days—independence days—in our country, you would have seen a strong feeling of independence, of pull-yourself-up-by-your-own-bootstraps mentality. That mentality helped get our country started. It helped us forge through the frontier and establish cities and places to live all across this country.) And America's desire and commitment to freedom are what makes our country democratic and really great.

But freedom has to be handled carefully. Freedom is not pure license to do whatever you want to do when you want to do it. If a free society is going to work, it has to have some laws, as you know from studying government. Sometimes as Christians we feel that because people are free to choose whatever religion they want, that means we should never "bug" others about the way they live or the way they talk, especially if they swear. Somehow speaking up for Christ doesn't fit with the way we do things in North America. It's really not "cool" at school. Speaking up for Christ means running the risk of losing a friend and being alienated—and as you well know, there's nothing worse than not having friends at school. It's the all-time worst thing that could ever happen to you. You know how hard you worked to get the chemistry right so that people will like you. And to speak up for Christ? No way!

The sad part is that sometimes it's even "not cool" to speak up for Christ in a lot of churches or youth groups today. For some reason, Christian young people think that being quiet is a virtue. So in the end, your friends in youth group don't talk a lot about Christ to one another. And since you know it's also not cool to do it at school, you end up never really speaking up for Christ.

There are some good reasons why you need to speak up for Jesus Christ and God. Once Jesus said this to his friends, "Anyone who is ashamed of me and my message in these days of unbelief and sin, I, the Messiah, will be ashamed of him when I return in the glory of my Father, with the holy angels" (Mark 8:38 TLB).

Heaven may seem like a big dream or a myth to you because you've never been there. But that's part of what it means to know Christ and walk by faith. Sure, you may never have experienced it, but heaven is real. And Christ was saying to His friends what He has said to friends all down through history, "Please don't be ashamed of me, I'm doing a lot for you in coming to earth and by going back to prepare a place for you. If you take the heat for a few years here on earth and take a little grief from people who make fun of you because you believe in me, it'll all pay off—somewhat on earth, but even more so in heaven."

Another place in the Bible, our friend Paul wrote:

> Be happy if you are cursed and insulted for being a Christian, for when that happens the Spirit of God will come upon you with great glory. Don't let me hear of your suffering for murdering or stealing or making trouble or being a busybody and prying into other people's affairs. But it is no shame to suffer for being a Christian. Praise God for the privilege of being in Christ's family and being called by his wonderful name!
>
> —1 PETER 4:14–15 TLB

There are places in this world where it is easier to be a Christian than here in North America. Not many places, but a few. But that is not really the point. It has *always* been hard for Christians to stand up for Christ, because we love to have friends. You know how important your friends are to you. Somehow we know inside that not all our friends are true friends. True friends will stick with you no matter what you believe, no matter if you are religious and know Christ or not.

It's hard to think about that, isn't it? Somehow, **we've come to believe that standing up for Christ means we'll be social misfits, total wimps, or weirdos.** Maybe you've known some Christians who have alienated all their friends. But that isn't Christ's idea at all about standing up for

Him. In fact, He expects you to have friends that don't know Him. That's the only way they'll ever hear about Him. But He expects you to be a person of conviction, too, and to stand up for Him at certain times. What are those times? Here are a few things you might consider.

Being ashamed of Christ means being quiet when someone curses. It means faking that you're not a Christian. It means acting different from what your conscience feels. It means not praying in public sometimes or sticking it to a friend who is slipping away from Christ. Being ashamed of Christ means not sharing Him with your friends and family right now.

But when you speak up for Christ, your life looks different. It means asking if a joke is "different" (*before* someone starts to tell it) and learning to walk away if it is. It means being free to pray in public every now and then for your meals. Or reading your Bible in public without being nervous and uptight about what other people will think of you. It means encouraging a friend who is doing something wrong. It means saying Christ is the answer when people say that life is relative or that the answer is to just do what you want to do or that no religion is the true religion.

If you are willing to be proud of Christ and willing to stand up for Him, look what good things can happen to you. The Bible says that if you're insulted because you know Christ, He will take care of you and bless you. The Bible says that it is no shame to suffer for being a Christian and that it is worse to suffer for doing things that aren't right, like murdering, stealing, making trouble, or gossiping. It's hard to believe, but *the pain of being rejected by your friends isn't nearly so bad as really making a mess of your life.*

A couple more things. Did you ever wonder why God said to speak up for Him? Surely God knows how important your friends are. The fact is, others need what you have. You need to have friends who don't know Christ. But you also need to stand up for what you believe. If you're weak and can't do that, then you need to be careful how much time you spend with people who don't know Christ and be careful what you do with them.

Another thing, when you have courage to speak up for Christ, you grow strong. But if you don't, you grow weak. God says that you're supposed to be the salt of the earth and the light in the darkness. Our world is dark; it is full of hurt and pain.

Think of the kids you know who have had abortions or who have messed up their lives with drugs or who have parents that are divorced. There is a lot of pain in this world, and God is looking to use someone who knows Him to bring some light into someone else's very dark life.

It's tough. So how do you do it? Here are a few ideas. First, grit your teeth, suck your gut in, and say, "God, with Your help I am going to stand up for You." Maybe you'll have to pray that prayer every day for a while, but God will honor it. He'll answer your prayer and honor it, and He'll help you stand up for Him.

Second, just blurt out what you know and believe. It may sound funny to you, but even if it sounds funny the way you say it or if it doesn't sound very religious or if it might not be the way your preacher says it, it is better to just blurt out what you believe than to hold it inside.

Third, practice. It takes practice to stand up for Christ. If you have baby brothers or sisters and have ever watched them learn to walk, you know it took them a lot of practice before they could quit crawling and learn to walk across the room. It's the same with you. In learning to stand up for Christ, you've got to do it once, then twice, then three times. And you'll soon learn who are your true friends—those who will stick with you. You'll also see how God can use you to help someone else who is hurting. The sad thing is that many Christians today don't even talk about Christ much, not in church, not in youth group, not amongst themselves. God never intended Christians to act like that. God is saying to you, "Speak up for Me at home, at church, with Christians, and without Christians. It may not be easy or comfortable, but it's the right thing to do. And by doing it, you'll be light in a dark world, and you'll grow strong yourself as you walk with Me."

Put this starting point in place in your life. Ask God to help you with it, and then see what good things He'll do through you.

16

Okay, here's the problem: Your mom and dad are divorced. You live with your mom, and life stinks sometimes. You miss your dad, but you feel guilty when you do. You think about getting married someday. For sure, you'll never get a divorce, right? That's probably what your mom said, too. Marriages don't even work on TV. At home there's never enough money. And you're supposed to believe there's hope for you to find the right person and be happy. For sure. Even if you did, you probably wouldn't be able to afford a house to live in. And even if you did, the odds are Russia will nuke us all. If there really is hope, where is it?

Life *is* rough sometimes. For some reason, everybody believes life was never meant to have hard spots. We believe life owes us a good time. Thrills, good sex, a great marriage, a great job, maybe a boat, and few worries. Sure, *other* people hurt, but not you.

Sometimes, though, life lays a heavy on you, and you get beat up. You know, you can work hard to keep yourself out of trouble—never speed or do drugs—but that doesn't guarantee that you're not going to hurt. You can live a clean life and still watch your parents divorce, get seriously ill, see your dad lose his job, break up with your girlfriend or boyfriend, or have your best friend move 1,000 miles away. Life can turn pretty sour at times.

When life doesn't deliver, we lose hope and want to give up. We feel like saying, "These heavies I can do without. It's checkout time."

Some people run away. They put a gun to their heads, lay down on the railroad tracks, or OD on drugs.

It's not always so messy. Some people will checkout in other ways. They'll "veg out." They'll get an average part-time job, do average school work, and watch a lot of average television.

Other people give up hope by doing dope. They smoke a joint just to get through the school day. One beer is never enough for them. You see them blasted or stoned at weekend parties.

Other people rationalize; they lie to themselves. They don't deal with reality very well. So when life turns tough, they blow it off and say it doesn't really hurt. Some pretty smart people, trying to handle pain on their own, do this.

When life hands you a bucket full of hurt and pain, you've got to know this:

STARTING POINT 16

There is always hope, even when life turns ugly.

That's right, there is *always* hope, no matter what happens. Did you ever feel like God doesn't know what He's doing with you? Maybe it's a SMALL hurt, like eating alone in the cafeteria, not being invited to a party, or running out of money and not being able to go with your youth group on a retreat. Or maybe it's a BIG hurt, like having a retarded sister or not getting along with your mom and dad. The fact is, no matter what size your problem is, there is always hope. You can believe that because God promised it—and He doesn't go back on what He says.

How you respond to this starting point is going to make a big difference in your destiny in life.

Let's look at a guy named Jeremiah. Jeremiah was a guy who basically talked tough to Jewish people thousands of years ago. He told the Jewish people to get their act together, to quit worshiping weird gods, to stop sleeping around and marrying women from other cultures. In general, he told them that they had forgotten God was in charge.

It's pretty easy to forget God is in charge. Good health, a great tan, a good family, enough food on the table, and a summer job make it tough to remember God is there.

But when things go bad, we start yelling for God. That's foxhole Christianity. When war breaks out and bullets whiz around us, then we turn to God.

But that doesn't really make a lot of sense. God wants to be our friend all the time.

Anyway, back to Jeremiah. Jeremiah wrote a letter. He didn't make a phone call, he didn't send a telegram, he didn't send a messenger. He wrote a letter to some Jews who were exiled. He wrote a letter to encourage them. (And you know this is how God communicates with you, too. He wrote you a letter, the Bible. It's not just another holy book in the world; it is a very personal letter written for you, to tell you there is always hope.)

Jeremiah's message from God to these people who were exiled was pretty simple. It went like this:

"For I know the plans I have for you," declares the LORD, "plans to prosper you and not to harm you, plans to give you hope and a future. Then you will call upon me and come and pray to me, and I will listen to you. You will seek me and find me when you seek me with all your heart."

—JEREMIAH 29:11–13 NIV

There it is in black and white. God made a commitment. Imagine, the God of the universe making a commitment to *you*. God has plans for you, for good and not for evil. How can that be, though, when you hurt? Because there is a difference in the way you *feel* about things and the way things really *are*. You're not alone or left out, even though you may feel that way sometimes. Things on the surface may look like there's no hope, but that's a matter of your perspective.

Some people see God and the devil in everything. If you pull a muscle before a big track meet, is that the devil or is it God? It all depends on how you see things. Just because we feel a certain way or we see things a certain way, doesn't mean that's the way things really are. We have to learn in life to look at things differently, to go *above* our feelings when it looks like there is no hope.

Why? Because God doesn't lie. And right in black and white He said there's always hope because He has plans for you for good, not for evil.

That means when you go home to one parent or your dad loses his job or your little sister is born retarded, God will turn those bad things into something good.

What happens when you lose hope in life? For one thing, you quit believing in the future. People who quit believing in the future end up causing more hurt than they had in the first place. You go too far with your date, because "it doesn't matter whether I'm a virgin or not." You smoke a joint. You play chicken in a car. You get depressed over grades. You fight a friend at the drop of a hat. When you lose hope, you quit believing in God. What you once believed about God, and about who He is, now seems like a myth. You don't feel God anymore; He seems far away.

But when you have hope, something awesome happens. Life really does begin to turn around. How do you have hope? For the good to come from these bad things, you have to meet three conditions. You can meet these conditions with a little effort.

1. Pray. Let's face it. Prayer is pretty mysterious. You can't see God, yet you can talk to Him. You can't explain prayer, but it works. God answers prayer. When you invited God to turn your life around, He did it. Even though you still struggle to live right, He really did start you down a new road. In the same way, God promises to listen and to answer your prayers. Sometimes it's yes, sometimes no, sometimes wait. But He always answers.

The great thing about knowing God is that you can talk to Him anywhere, anytime. Try this experiment sometime. When you're going somewhere on your bike, on foot, or in the car—pray. Ask God specifically for what you need. You'll find out He'll listen. He promised to. Sure, it's a mystery, but that doesn't change the fact that it really happens.

Remember God said to Jeremiah, "Then you will call upon me [God]. . . . You will seek me and find me when you seek me with all your heart."

It's possible to look for God in all the wrong places. Some people look in weird cults, meditation, or some mystical experience. The fact is, God is much easier to find. The hope He gives is yours by just opening your mouth and talking to Him.

2. Believe what the Bible says. Ask God to help you believe in the plan He has for you. Ask God to help you think differently about the way He works with you.

You see, God doesn't intend for you to have a rotten life. He intends for you to have a good life. Keep this in mind: God is motivated by love, and not by fear, anger, or bitterness. *Ever*. If you could get a picture fixed in your mind, it ought to be this one: God has His arm around you, all the time, every step of the way in your life. He never has your arm twisted behind your back, trying to get you to do something. He never is ready to pounce on you if you mess up.

3. Work on your attitude. When you hurt, you don't see clearly. Nobody does. You feel down. That's when it's hard to see that God really does care.

That's when you need to talk straight to yourself like an adult. It's not enough to just bounce off walls based on how you feel. Go with the facts the

Bible says are real and true. The fact is, God knows you and He does have a plan for you. And it's not a plan to destroy you; it's a plan to give you a good future.

There's always hope with God. All hurt passes. No matter how big your hurt is, it eventually goes away. Some good things are going to happen in your life.

If you believe what Jeremiah said, nothing will ever knock you down forever. Sure, you'll get knocked down. But not forever. If you believe God has a good plan for you, small things won't get to you. And because of that, life will go better. You'll see that some things you used to think were pretty important aren't as important as you thought. Because in the flow of God's plan for your life, small hurts pass soon away.

Every hurt in your life can be an asset if you keep the right attitude about God. You can turn any problem in your life into an asset, into something very valuable, if you have the right attitude. The right attitude is simply this: God loves you, has His arm around you, and is committed to your best. When you believe there's always hope, you'll hold on to the things that are really important. A lot of people give up a lot of important things because they lose hope.

In a thousand ways you can give up important things in life. You can throw away your virginity. You can throw away your career. You can throw away an opportunity to go to the college of your choice. You can throw away a good relationship with your parents or a good friendship.

So, here's your starting point: There is always hope. This is one starting point you can put to work anytime. It is never, ever too late, *no matter what has happened to you in life*. God is in the habit of helping people start over, every day. The hope you need is within your reach if you just ask God for it. You'll see. He'll deliver!

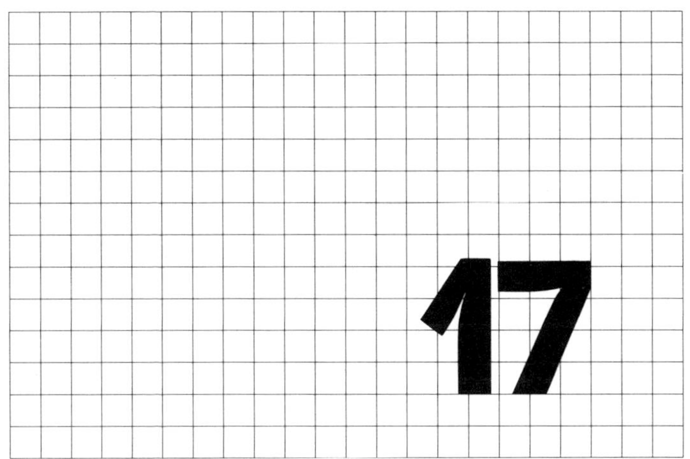

If you believe everything you see and hear on TV, the school principal, geometry teacher, Sunday school teacher, preacher, everybody on your block, everybody in the junior class at high school, the president, the pope, and Margaret Thatcher are all having sex 24 hours a day—and loving it.

Okay, tell the truth. Is this the first chapter you are reading in this book? If so, you passed the test! You're normal. Even if you didn't turn here first, we all know that just about anything that has the word *sex* in it has a certain way of attracting our attention. It makes people read magazines under blankets at night with flashlights. It turns our heads when we see it written on anything. So, here it is. This is the good stuff. The big one. This is the chapter you've been waiting for.

At the risk of repeating something you already know, let's get one card out on the table. Sex feels great. In fact, sex feels so great that it gets a lot of people into trouble. That's why you need to get this starting point burned into your mind or branded on your right hand.

STARTING POINT 17

Be careful what sexual baggage you pick up.

How can something that seems so good and so much fun be such a big problem? Can you figure that out? Actually, God figured it out a long time ago. But let's wait a minute before we talk about what He has to say.

You've probably heard the church's party line at least a hundred times before, haven't you? "Flee youthful lusts." (What in the world is a youthful lust anyway?) Or, "Stay away from dirty magazines and movies." "Stay a virgin." "Think pure thoughts." All of those are pretty good pieces of advice. But *you* know the truth better than anyone— advice is much easier given than followed.

These things are usually said by parents and people who don't live where you live today. They don't live in the locker room or in the school or in the movie theaters. In fact, if you're a teenager today, you have the hardest battle of all times. At no time in history has it ever been more difficult to figure out what you are supposed to do about sex.

In fact, it seems that parents, preachers, and Sunday school teachers often just don't understand where you are.

You live in a tough world. Nowadays, it seems that what's cool is to be responsible. The issue isn't whether you have sex or not, it's "protect yourself with contraceptives." (Wow, how adult.) Or, it's not whether you go all the way, it's "have sex when the time is right for you." (According to whose clock?) Or, "If you love the person it's okay." (Okay with whom?)

But let's talk about some very important truths for a minute. There are seven laws of sex you might as well get straight in your life and accept, because they are *not* going to change.

Law 1: Sex outside marriage is wrong. (Translated into modern language, that law reads like this: Sex outside marriage is wrong.)

Sometimes you'll hear your friends say when it comes to sex, "It's my life, I can do with it what I want. As long as I don't hurt anyone, whatever I do is okay." But sex is never a solo performance. Even if you masturbate, your sexuality is almost always linked with another person. That's why it's important for you to understand at your age that the only responsible sex is sex *inside* marriage.

What a pain! Don't you hate to hear that? Just

when you get old enough to enjoy some things in life, someone comes along and says something like that.

Here's what God has to say about sex in marriage:

> It is God's will that you should be holy; that you should avoid sexual immorality [sex outside marriage]; that each of you should learn to control his own body in a way that is holy and honorable, not in passionate lust like the heathen, who do not know God; and that in this matter no one should wrong his brother or take advantage of him. The Lord will punish men for all such sins, as we have already told you and warned you. For God did not call us to be impure, but to live a holy life.
>
> —1 THESSALONIANS 4:3–7 NIV

What can you add to that?

Law 2: It *does* matter if you are a virgin when you get married. Think about this. Only the people who are virgins when they get married will ever really know how great sex is because they stayed a virgin. Some people today say being a virgin doesn't matter, that if you are playing around a lot and doing everything but having sex, you might as well do it. In one sense, that's true. Cutting it as close to the edge as you can without actually "doing it" is stretching the concept of being a virgin. That's playing games with words and isn't what God meant when He said control your body in a way that is holy.

In another sense, almost having sex and having

it are two different things. God expects something different from you if you are a Christian. And it is not just that He expects it—He asks it of you because He knows what's good for you. Thousands and thousands of people who waited to have sex for the first time when they were married are really the only ones who can tell you how great sex is because they waited.

You'll be lucky if you find 1 in 10 of your friends who feel that way, but that doesn't make them right. Nor does it make the messages you hear and the rock videos you see right, either. It does matter if you are a virgin. It matters because someone else is depending on you to make good choices about sex. Believe it or not, someday you will fall in love with somebody you will marry. If that person has been waiting to have sex inside marriage, then there will be a huge hurt and disappointment and an obstacle you will have to overcome together.

Sure it's tough to say no, and it's tough to say no over and over again each time you go out with somebody new. But if you can hold on to your values until you get married, you'll find there will be a lot less hurt and a lot fewer stumbling blocks to overcome. That's hard to remember when you are with someone who looks and feels good to you when you hug each other and curl up together. But if you can remember to hold on to your values in the heat of the moment, you'll save yourself an awful lot of heartache later.

Law 3: It *doesn't* matter if you stay a vir-

gin. What?! How can it matter and then *not* matter? Here's why. Some of you who are reading this have already messed up. You've gone too far. In fact, you've gone all the way. Maybe only once, maybe five times, maybe twenty times. You know what? This is the hardest and most confusing thing to understand. But if you've never had sex, it's important not to. And if you ever have had sex, it's important not to do it again until you're married—no matter what your past is or how much you care about the person.

Most people who have had sex would tell those who haven't, "Wait, it wasn't worth it." "The good feelings only lasted a small amount of time, and then I really began to feel guilty." "I couldn't believe how much I hurt emotionally afterwards." "No one ever told me it would be like this." "I thought there would be a lot more fun involved."

So often, a tremendous amount of pain and hurt comes with having sex before marriage, especially when you break up with someone you care about. But God has a wonderful and good plan for your life—even when you mess up sexually. The Bible says, "If we confess our sins, He is faithful and just and will forgive us our sins and purify us from all unrighteousness" (1 John 1:9 NIV).

You know what that means? God can make you a virgin again in your mind and in your heart. He can heal the scars. That is what He promised in His word. And that's why it's confusing. If you've never had sex, God warns you to stay a virgin. But if you have, He'll be there to pick up the pieces and to bring healing. The road of sexual mistakes is a long one that you do not have to travel. It is a road of bad memories and hurt emotions that God has to heal. He can't do that unless you ask Him and are willing to give up the kinds of sexual behavior that got you into trouble in the first place. It's complicated. Sometimes healing takes a long time. Sometimes you never fully heal. That's why it *does* matter if you are a virgin at the same time it *doesn't* matter, because of what God will do for you.

Law 4: Sex outside of marriage is governed by a law of diminishing returns. Let's talk about some basic arithmetic here. Very few people go out on a first date and suddenly rip off all their clothes and have raving, passionate sex without giving a thought for the other person. Sure, that might happen in some singles' bars in the movies. But more often than not, people who got in trouble started simply by escalating what they did with each other's bodies.

There is something about sex that eats you up. You crave more and more sex, and you crave to be satisfied. Holding hands might be enough jollies for you for one or two dates, but then it takes more. And one kiss isn't enough, but it takes two or three to make you feel satisfied sexually. That's the law of diminishing returns, and the only place that it ends is full-fledged sex.

The law of diminishing returns is a law you can't change. It's bigger than you. You might try to bend it by inventing some halfway points. But God never intended those halfway points to be there. What God really intended was for you to have full satisfaction with sex, and the only time you are ever fully satisfied is when you are married to someone.

Law 5: Every new set of sexual experiences with a new person hardens you in some small way. While it's true that God can forgive you and heal your memories and emotions, every time you have a new sexual experience with someone, your life changes. You give up a little piece of innocence; you give up a piece of your heart.

And do you know what that's called? Picking up sexual baggage. People who have a multitude of sexual experiences with a lot of different people, from the time they're fourteen or fifteen years old until they are thirty and get married, end up carrying around a heavy load of memories and guilt. Each new experience is another bag they pick up and try to carry. It weighs them down in their heart, and they're never free to be who they were intended to be.

Law 6: What you think sexually will ultimately show up in how you live. Here's what the Bible has to say about that: "But each one is tempted when, by his own evil desire, he is dragged away and enticed. Then, after desire has conceived, it gives birth to sin; and sin, when it is full-grown gives birth to death" (James 1:14–15 NIV).

Now, look at that. Where do evil desires start? Between your legs? No way. They start in your mind; they start with what you think about. The end result is that you make bad choices about how you live. God calls those bad choices sin. But that sin started with how you think.

One way to avoid picking up sexual baggage in life is to guard your thoughts. Do you want to guard your thoughts? Walk away from a dirty joke. When you go to the 7-Eleven to buy groceries for your mom, don't even look at the covers of dirty magazines. When you lie in bed at night or in the morning, keep a good book or a good magazine beside your bed. And most of all, ask God to help you.

Law 7: If you really love yourself, you'll guard yourself sexually. Here's what the Bible says:

> Flee from sexual immorality. All other sins a man commits are outside his body, but he who sins sexually sins against his own body. Do you not know that your body is a temple of the Holy Spirit [God], who is in you, whom you have received from God? You are not your own; you were bought at a price. Therefore honor God with your body.
>
> —1 CORINTHIANS 6:18–20 NIV

People talk a lot today about taking care of their bodies and keeping them in good shape. Then they turn right around and let other people touch them and do whatever they want to their bodies. Isn't it interesting that to God sexual sin is a sin that you commit against your own body? It's like punching yourself on purpose or breaking your own leg. It does not make sense. If you're in your right mind, you wouldn't do those things. Yet, that's what sexual sins are. They are sins and hurts and pains against your own body. And if you really care about yourself and respect yourself, you are going to be careful about what you do sexually.

In the end, all the choices about sex, such as how far you go with your date on a Friday night, really come down to you—how much character you have, what you believe, and how much you believe what God's Word says about sex.

Nobody with any brains is going to tell you that it is easy. That's why it comes back to you. You can't blame the rock videos, your parents, the sex education class, or your boyfriend or girlfriend.

It all comes back to you and how committed you are to doing what is right before God. Being committed to purity is perhaps the hardest thing you will have to do. But *you* have to come to the conclusion for *you* that being pure is best.

If you are not settled on purity, you will find yourself saying things like "I can handle sex." "We love each other." "Surely, God can't mean that we can't touch each other." "Honestly, it feels too good to quit."

All interesting ideas, but not very adult. Do you want to be an adult? Then you are going to have to act like one. Mature adults know how to say no to a lot of different things. They know how to be tough.

And here's why getting this starting point in place in your life is important. *Every piece of sexual baggage you pick up makes it tougher and tougher to say no.*

But when you don't pick up sexual baggage along the way, you are going to have good feelings about yourself. You'll feel that you're okay, that you have nothing to hide. You will feel like an adult who has the ability to say no.

Being careful not to pick up sexual baggage means that you will have good feelings about other people, too. You will begin to see people not as just warm bodies to serve your needs, but as whole people who have a lot to contribute to your life. You will see sex as the good experience God intended it to be in your life. You will see sex not as feelings He wants to repress and take away from you, but as feelings He wants you to guard so that when you get married they can spring out and come alive in ways you never dreamed possible.

And one more thing, by not picking up sexual baggage throughout life, you are going to eliminate some more places where you could mess up your life: surprise babies, marriages because you have to, or pain from abortions.

God's good plan is for you to be a whole person. God gave you those feelings you get when you are near somebody you care about, but He left you the responsibility to guard them.

Are you struggling with sex? Ask God for help.

Do you realize in today's world you will *never ever* win without His help? Nice-looking, easy-to-get-in-bed girls and guys are everywhere.

Face facts. Sex is bigger than you are. Without God's help, you are not going to make it. Talk to your parents, take a friend into your confidence, or call a friend before a date to pray with you.

Sound hokey? How bad do you want to win?

A lot of people struggle with masturbation, with going too far on a date, and with reading dirty magazines. Talk to your parents about it or talk with your preacher. Do you realize that even though they come from a different generation they really do care about you and want what is best for you? Asking them to pray for you when you are struggling with sex may sound weird, but it also may save you an awful lot of trouble.

Another thought. Keep your failures in perspective. Hair isn't going to grow on the palms of your hands and your eyes won't fall out every time you make a sexual mistake. God will help you and forgive, but don't take advantage of His forgiveness, either. God is not exactly someone you want to take advantage of.

Don't get fooled by rationalization. Yes, you might love somebody and feel that you have to be with that person. And sometimes when you are alone, your mind will probably tell you there can't be anything wrong with taking care of your own sexual needs. But think twice! Those thoughts might be rational but that does not make them right.

Make a point to pray and ask God regularly what He wants you to do. And then live by it. God will never steer you against what He wrote in the Bible. If you don't ever hear God's voice, don't let that stop you from doing what is right. Go back and read some of the verses that are at the beginning of this chapter. They'll help you see what God really wants you to do.

And last, some practical advice. Keep your clothes on, zipped up and buttoned up. Ask God for His strength, and you'll leave a lot of sexual baggage behind you.

Every adult you know bugs you to tell the truth. And they're more curious about everything you do than the CIA, KGB, and FBI all put together. You can't sneeze or be gone ten minutes too long to the john in school without somebody checking up on you.

Do you ever feel that everyone is watching you? That everyone expects you to be perfect? How do you handle that?

Under pressure, you can do a lot of things you don't really feel are right. When it comes to saving your hide, sometimes it seems that telling a lie is the way to go. There's something about telling a lie, even a small one, that's like quicksand. You lie about going to a friend's house to study when you're really going to a concert. But when you lie, it's often the *second* lie that gets you in trouble. It's the one you tell to cover up for being late because the concert went longer than you thought. So instead of telling one lie, you end up telling two. That's 100 percent more than you thought you'd tell, and that's what makes telling lies like quicksand—lies just keep sucking you in further and further.

There's got to be a better way. There is, and it's this:

STARTING POINT 18

Tell the truth in everything.

Okay, this is Sunday School 101, right? Everybody knows you're supposed to tell the truth. Right. Then why is it so many people don't tell the truth? Why do your friends in school lie to their parents about where they are on Friday nights?

Hey, look around the next time a test is given at school. You'll see people with cheat sheets on their shoes, underneath their test papers, and written on the palms on their hands. Why do so many people cheat?

We all know we should be honest. Ask people you run into on the street. They'll tell you being honest is important. Today, though, people's values are changing. It used to be that a lot of people in our country believed they should tell the truth in everything. But now telling the truth comes out something like this, "It's okay not to be truthful so long as no one gets hurt." That means if you have to tell a lie and everything works out okay, you win.

So, if you lie to your parents and go to a rock concert instead of studying and you get a B on your test, then everything is cool. That's relativity. And we've talked about that. When it comes to what you believe in life, relativity just doesn't cut it. That's why this starting point is so important.

Telling the truth in everything means having integrity. Being a person of integrity means your actions in public *and* in private reflect who you *really* are. If you have integrity, your walk matches your talk. People can judge you by your actions. They know when they see you in action, they see the real you.

Integrity means acting as if God is always with you and always sees everything you do, both in public and private. Sometimes it's easy to get fooled into thinking you're by yourself when you lie in bed and it's all quiet and dark. Or believing nobody can see what you do when you're in a car with your date. But a person of integrity behaves the same way in private and in public. God, your parents, or your date could walk in on you at any time and say, "Hey, that's someone I know, someone I'm proud to be with." That's a tall order when you stop to think of it. Think back over the last week or two.

Could somebody have watched how you behaved with your last date, or how you behaved alone in the bathroom, and said, "Hey, that's someone I'm proud of"?

Now here's something important to catch. *The same God you want to have with you when you're down or afraid, is also there in private with you when you're struggling to do the right thing.* God is everywhere, and He sees everything—including when people say one thing and do another.

If you've been in the habit of covering up for yourself, maybe it's time to make a change. Start by being honest with God. If you want to do something really stupid, try to fool God by not coming clean with Him. Pretend He doesn't see the attitude you have towards your parents, or how you act when you're in private. God is the first person to be honest with if you want to be a person of integrity. Believe it or not, God wants to hear from you, even when you mess up, even when you fail Him and yourself. That's just the way God is.

Somehow we think God doesn't want to hear from us after we've made mistakes. Just the opposite is true. God wants to hear from you any time, whether you're right or wrong. He already knows what you've been doing before you even talk to Him. The point is, God wants you to bring your problems to Him. Because that's what builds a friendship with Him. God is, in many ways, lonely. He wants to hear from you. He wants to hear about your thoughts and dreams, your disappointments and your failures. That's the way He has chosen to talk to you and help you win the next time.

If you're going to be a person of integrity, the second person you've got to be honest with is yourself. A really stupid thing to do is to try to rationalize away who you are. Sometimes people aren't honest with themselves about their abilities, and so they add to themselves. You can spot these people a mile away. They walk with their nose a little higher and act as if they're the greatest thing since sliced white bread. They're the ones who are too cool to talk to you in public, but who will talk to you when they're down or lonely, as long as none of their friends are looking.

Sometimes when you're a teenager it's easy to feel you have nothing to offer the world. You look at your body and you're either too thin or too fat. You've got zits sometimes. Your grades are bad sometimes. You don't even know who you are some days or where you're headed. Those are the days it's easy to lie to yourself and think, *Hey, I'm worth nothing.* That's when teenagers turn to drugs or booze or even think about killing themselves because they think there's nothing to live for.

Actually, they minimize their own worth because they don't really see what good things they have to offer the world. That gets a lot of teenagers in trouble today. It makes girls have sex with guys to prove they're lovable. It makes guys get drunk at parties to be one of the boys. Tell yourself the truth. You *are* worth something because of the good things God has put in you and done for you—even if they're hard to see sometimes.

Finally, if you're going to be a person of integrity, you've got to be honest with everybody elsc around you. Sometimes we think having friends is the most important thing in life, but you know what? *Being honest is more important than having friends.* And you're better off being true to yourself, because someday you could find yourself down the road with a lot of friends, none of them telling the truth, and then realize you're surrounded by people you can't really trust.

The Bible says to tell the truth in everything. Stand up for what you believe. Don't cheat on the little things of life, like accepting a stolen cassette from a friend, jumping the fence at a football game, or asking somebody who just took a test what one of the questions is. Those are small ways to be honest, but they all add up to become really important.

The Bible has some good thoughts about being honest. Listen to these:

> Do not have two differing weights in your bag—one heavy, one light. Do not have two differing measures in your house—one large, one small. You must have accurate and honest weights and measures, so that you may live long in the land the LORD your God is giving you. For the LORD your God detests anyone who does these things, anyone who deals dishonestly.
>
> —DEUTERONOMY 25:13–16 NIV

Those verses say, "Don't have a double standard." Don't expect the wife to be a virgin if the husband is not prepared to be one. Don't insist that your parents be fair with you, if you're not going to be fair with them. That's what it means to be a person of integrity, to measure yourself and others by the same standard without rationalizing. God Himself said, "Don't rationalize."

God wasn't trying to lay down some heavy law that would be hard for you to follow. No, He knows something about human nature. **God knows that if you make a practice of telling the truth, you'll have better relationships, peace of mind, and a lot fewer complications in life.**

When your starting point isn't to be a person of integrity, you begin to drift just a little bit, not a whole lot at once. You don't go out and get drunk one Friday night and then tell your parents you were studying with friends. No, you start with a little lie. It's the little dent in the fender that you claim you knew nothing about when your parents ask you. It's not really being straight with your parents when they ask you what kind of movie you saw.

It's not the big lies but the little ones that draw you away from walking closely with God and being honest with God and yourself. Your values slip just a little bit, maybe 10 percent. Then you know what happens? You begin to get suspicious about other people. When you're not a person of integrity, you don't trust others because *you* know you really aren't honest.

You tend to look at others the way you look at yourself. You know you're not honest, so why would anybody else be that way? And then the big double standard comes in. You do things in private, but deny it or act real pious in church. You know what that's like—to go to church on Sunday and act like you're really into the sermon, knowing that what is being said applies to you.

In the end, you end up rationalizing things that you once thought were bad, but now think, *Hey, if nobody gets hurt, it's alright.* All of that comes about because your starting point wasn't to be a person of integrity.

Now let's be realistic. The likelihood of your getting thrown in jail for cheating on your income taxes or being convicted of stealing seems pretty remote. After all, you know God. You go to church, you're a good person, you try to read the Bible, and hey look, you're even reading a religious book like this. But you know what? You can be as phony as a three-dollar bill by not being honest with your God, yourself, and those around you.

Altogether, the little white lies and double standards hurt you in the end. That's why God says not to have double standards. God knew if you had one set of weights, you wouldn't have to juggle the truth or cover your trail. And somehow, being honest even when it hurts works out better for you in every way. Now let's wrap this up and go right back to where we started.

It is a jungle out there; a lot of people expect you to be perfect. And sometimes, let's face it, you're going to mess up. That's when you're going to be tempted to tell a lie to cover your tracks. Even though it's tough, listen to that little voice inside of you that says, *Hey, tell the truth.* That voice is actually God's voice. It's actually God's Spirit telling you to be careful, to be honest.

Watch for ways you might be slipping. Ask God to help you with the white lies and double standards in your life. Choose to walk away from a joke you don't believe is right. Speak up when someone takes God's name in vain. Don't cheat on *any* tests. Tell the truth about why you're late or if the movie you saw was more raunchy than you thought it would be. Be careful what you do in private. It'll be tough at the time, don't kid yourself. But in the long run, every day you're honest is going to add good things to your life, give you more peace than you ever could imagine, and a life that will have God's favor.

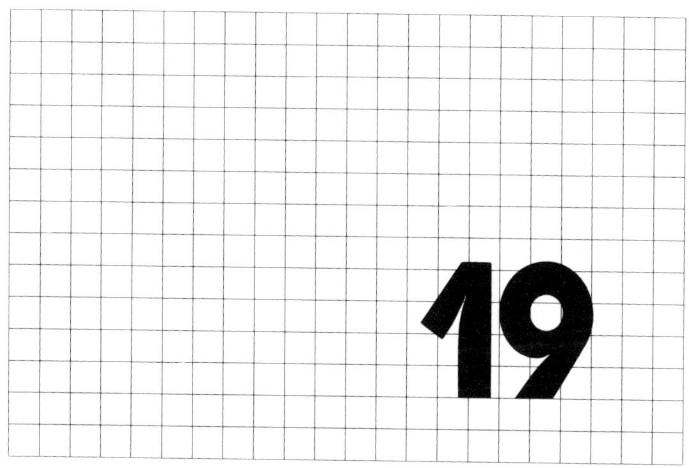

19

In eighth and ninth grades the plague is worse than in seventh grade. Now not only what you wear is important, but where you go, who your friends are, and who you are seen with in the cafeteria. In tenth and eleventh grades, all this *and* what summer job you'll have, who your friends are, what groups you belong to in school, and what music you listen to.

And then twelfth grade hits. The big decision: What school will you go to? And what will your friends think if you choose the wrong school or do the wrong thing after high school? Finally, you've got it all pieced together. It's your senior year, and you realize, hey, you've been making the right choices—you do have some style.

Then disaster strikes. You graduate. All those hours of trying to have some style, all the panic of trying to show up at the right place in the right outfit, are suddenly all gone at graduation.

The good news is, there's nothing wrong with having style and trying to put some style and color in your life. The bad news is, there's more to life than owning your own Bruce Springsteen album or having a certain color Reeboks. If those things occupy most of your time and energy, you're going to find yourself someday in the ball game of life with the score 10–0 and *not* on the winning team. That's why you've got to have the right starting point when it comes to style.

STARTING POINT 19

Remember, things that count come before having style.

It's really easy to get fooled on this one when everybody around you is screaming to have style. Hey, let's be realistic. Style's important. You probably wish your parents realized that more. Parents can be thick-headed sometimes, can't they? They don't realize that all tennis shoes were *not* created equal, that "blue" jeans *do* come in more than one color, a haircut is not a *haircut,* all rock 'n' roll groups don't play exactly the same songs, and just because somebody from your algebra class lives next door doesn't make you best friends.

But let's stop and think for a moment. As a card-carrying member (with a brain) of the human race, how really important is style to you? Maybe it's time to rethink your style. Some Christians might tell you God doesn't care about style. For a long time many Christians thought anything that had to do with style was not right before God. So they wore plain clothing and built plain churches. Yet God has given us some striking examples of style in nature.

Fruit trees bloom all different colors in the spring. Leaves turn colors in the fall. From seashells to the designs on a frog's back to the human body, God's handiwork shows He's greatly concerned about style. Think about music. God has given the world all kinds of music that creates different moods in us when we hear it. Anybody who said that God didn't care about style is really out of it. God made a very beautiful world that has a tremendous amount of style in it: Birds that sing, even talk. Waves on the beach. Thunderstorms. Lizards that change colors. Bugs that light up at night. Caterpillars that become butterflies.

But you see, it all comes down to priorities. While God is very concerned about style and demonstrated it in the created world, it wasn't the most important thing on His mind. That means it probably ought not to be the most important thing on your mind, either. You've got to have the right starting point. Things of substance, things that count, have to come before matters of style. By putting this important starting point in place in your life, you're going to save yourself an awful lot of hassles.

A number of people are concerned about improving themselves—that's good. It's good to want to be a sharp person, but you can take it too far. You know what it's like to get up in the morning and feel great pressure to choose the right thing to wear. You know you're too concerned about style when you stretch your budget or modesty quotient just so that you make the "right" appearance. You know something is shallow about your life when *looking* good is more important to you than *being* good.

Being too caught up in style and appearances shows up another way—in how you treat your friends. If other people's feelings get hurt because you don't say hello to them when you're with the "in" people, something is wrong in your life. Bragging about what you did last weekend or putting someone down to make yourself look good are proofs that style is too important to you.

When you put style ahead of things that count, some bad things begin to happen in your life. You get bent out of shape over little things. If somebody doesn't compliment you on your Reeboks, or you don't get invited to a certain party, it bothers you. You can get too dependent on other peoples' opinions of you and begin to shape your values and make your decisions based on what others will think.

Here is a good piece of advice to remember: *If you make your most important decisions about life based on what other people think, you are going to buy yourself a shopping bag full of trouble.* God expects you to learn to value His opinion more than others to learn things that count—like how to love, forgive, have faith, and walk with God, even when it's inconvenient or unpopular.

Jesus had some good thoughts about style and substance. They go something like this:

Do not store up for yourselves treasures on earth, where moth and rust destroy, and where thieves break in and steal. But store up for yourselves treasures in heaven, where moth and rust do not destroy, and where thieves do not break in and steal. For where your treasure is, there your heart will be also. The eye is the lamp of the body. If your eyes are good, your whole body will be full of light. But if your eyes are bad, your whole body will be full of darkness. If then the light within you is darkness, how great is that darkness! No one can serve two masters. Either he will hate the one and love the other, or he will be devoted to the one and despise the other. You cannot serve both God and Money.

—MATTHEW 6:19–24 NIV

Those verses say you could spend your whole life storing up the treasure of what other people think of you, other people's opinions. But in a second, like graduation, all those opinions don't count anymore. You could move away your junior year of school. All those years you were trying to do things in style would be blown away. In another place, you would have to start all over your junior and senior years.

It's tough to understand Jesus' meaning, especially when everyone seems to say that going in style is most important, that having everything your own way is what counts. Jesus comes along and says something entirely different. He says not to be so concerned about what you wear, what you eat, and who you're seen with. Storing up the treasure of what others think of you won't make you rich. Jesus says your priorities have got to be different, you've got to focus on things that God says count.

The Bible says in one place that a person who follows God's way (who focuses on things that count) is like a tree along a riverbank bearing delicious fruit each season. If you're going to be that person, the roots of your life have to go deep into God's Word. And that means spending time with God. It means pressing on towards things that count. It means putting less importance on how you're dressed or who your friends are.

The only thing that matters in life is who you *really* are—not the vapor trail you leave behind. What keeps a jet flying is its engines. They're the power that drives the jet, not the smoke they leave behind.

One final thought: **Being right in life is more important than just looking right.** A lot of thinking today goes like this: "Sex in a bed with clean sheets in a nice hotel room is okay, as long as you're dressed in style." Or, "It doesn't really matter what you believe as long as you've got a job that pays well and lets you finance what you want to do on the weekend." This kind of thinking is wrong. Dead wrong. It's not the way God says to live. God has a better idea. He says, "Do things that count in life."

Yeah, God has style. Just look around you. But God also is more concerned about whether people would live forever than He was about the rest of His creation. God's best creation was people, and that's where He has focused His attention down through history.

The vapor trail you leave behind in life is not what's important. What really matters in life is who you are inside, not the impression you leave.

Start being a person of substance. Do things that count, that make you a better Christian. Why not sit home one night with your family instead of running off to a movie? Do something kind this week for someone—in secret. Take a few extra minutes to read your Bible a little longer. Take a morning this week and read the newspaper. Clean up your room without being asked. Do the dishes one night without moaning. Pray on your knees today. Ask God to open your eyes to help you achieve balance in your life.

God doesn't expect you to give up wanting to look good and dress well. He doesn't ask you to give up wanting to have friends. But God does want you to be balanced. He wants you to put the things that count ahead of style in your life. Ask God to open your eyes to things that really count. He'll help you find just the right balance between style and things that count.

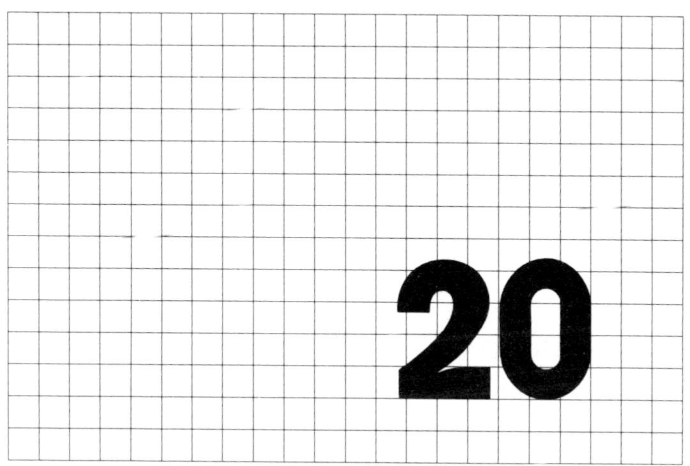

About the only thing worse than not having money would be spending the rest of your life without being allowed to put on a pair of jeans and tennis shoes.

Don't you love the feeling of having money in your pocket? It makes you feel a little less dependent on your parents or your friends. Having a good part-time job so you can buy a nice ten-speed or tickets to a concert makes all the hours you work worthwhile.

Money's a great thing to have, isn't it? Life can be the pits without it. As great as money is, it's a challenge to handle it right. And that's why you need this starting point in your life.

STARTING POINT 20

Hold loosely to things in your life.

It's hard to think that a ten-speed bike, a Walkman personal cassette player, a pair of skis, an old car, and your records can hurt you in life, but they can. You're growing up in a country where owning things and getting ahead is not just acceptable, it's *expected* of you.

It costs a lot of money to be somebody these days in school, doesn't it? There's a lot of pressure on you to buy the right pair of jeans or see a movie just as soon as it's released—no matter how much it costs. TV says it. Magazines say it. Your friends say it. Maybe even your parents say it. You need money, and lots of it, to "be somebody."

But is that really true? Just because all those people say it and live as if luxury items and expensive entertainment are their God-given due, does that make it right?

Outside of sex, there is no greater pressure on you as a young person than to become a full-blown, first-class, certified, card-carrying materialist. After seeing 1,000 commercials for cars, makeup, clothes, movies, Miller Lite, and 65,000 other goodies, how can you help but believe that owning nice things is important? Next time you walk through a mall, look around. It's like going to a giant pep rally where all the merchandise are screaming, "Buy Me! Choose Me! Own Me!"

Some Christians aren't much help in this area. A lot of preachers on television say, "Don't tell God you want a Cadillac, tell Him what color you want." They say to you, "God wants you rich!"

Surprise. Whether it's your preacher, your mom and dad, or your best friend, no matter who says it to you, it's absolutely untrue that God wants you financially rich. What God wants is for you to learn to hold loosely to things in life, because He knows the power of possessions in people's lives.

People in the United States, Canada, and a number of countries in Europe consume more, live ten times more comfortably, and are cared for better than the rest of the world where three times as many people live. Now, you can't help *where* you were born, but you can help *how you live* since you've been born. It isn't bad to make good money if your first goal is to share what you earn. Being a good investor and guardian of what God gives you is what the Lord expects.

Jesus told the story of a man who buried his money and never invested it—that was the wrong way to handle his money. The man who invested his money carefully, and earned interest ten times over, was the man God really honored—and that's what God expects from us. You've probably heard your parents say, "Finish what's on your plate, there are starving people in Africa." To which you reply, "Then let's box these brussels sprouts up and send them to them." If it was that easy, people wouldn't be starving.

But our world is full of injustice. Good people, just like you and your parents, live in Africa today and are starving to death, just because they happen to have been born in the wrong country.

Now you can't solve all the problems of injustice, but you can live right. You can handle your money in a way that pleases God. Here's a thought:

> But godliness with contentment is great gain. For we brought nothing into the world, and we can take nothing out of it. But if we have food and clothing, we will be content with that. People who want to get rich fall into temptation and a trap and into many foolish and harmful desires that plunge men into ruin and destruction. For the love of money is a root of all kinds of evil. Some people, eager for money, have wandered from the faith and pierced themselves with many griefs.
>
> —1 TIMOTHY 6:6–10 NIV

That's the real truth. Your possessions can control you. Just ask your parents that. Ask them if it's a struggle to spend their money wisely. You'll find, if they're honest with you, that it's a struggle for them to not let the things they own, like their house or their car, consume all their time and energy.

Unfortunately, a lot of people live Monday through Friday and work long, hard hours just to finance their weekend. God never intended for *anyone,* including your parents, to live that way no matter what the yuppies and their friends say. That kind of attitude comes from letting possessions become more important than people and God. Those Bible verses aren't talking about saving up for a ten-speed bike or new clothes; they're saying that wanting to get rich can really foul up your life. Christians who desire to get rich and be comfortable often end up wandering away from God.

You've got to have your priorities straight. The right order is that God and people come before possessions. If you didn't get those Reeboks, designer jeans, or the makeup you think you just have to have, what's the worst thing that would happen to you? Would you die? If you missed your lunch today with some friends because you didn't have money to go to McDonald's with them, is that the end of your friendship with them? The end of the world? See, the fact is, you can survive quite well. **Nothing bad is going to happen to you if you don't get certain things that you feel like you just absolutely have to have.**

It takes a lot of money to be somebody these days if you go by the world's standards. But those standards aren't God's. God says the truly happy people are those who walk with Him and are contented with their circumstances. You want to learn how to hold loosely to things in life? Here are some things you can do:

1. Next time you buy some clothes, do it on a little less money, even if that means buying

them at a discount store. Then give the difference to your church. It won't be the end of the world to own some things that didn't come from the "best" shop in the mall.

2. Take some money you saved and buy something nice for a needy friend. Take your folks out for a meal and pick up the tab. If you want to know whether things control you, see if you can give money away. One of the best ways to break the grip of possessions on you and your life is to give them away or let somebody else borrow them. Try giving above and beyond what you normally give to your church.

3. Be honest with yourself and others. How important are your possessions to you? Wanting to collect and own a lot of nice things disappoints God. He never intended for these possessions to take that high a place in your life. Talk to your parents. A lot of parents today believe providing you with a nice home and all the latest clothes is important. Ask them where they are when it comes to possessions.

More and more in our country, being wealthy and comfortable is the goal of most people. It takes the place of learning to live on less, sharing with others, and pursuing things that last forever. The cold, hard facts are that all people die eventually and take a big goose egg with them. God doesn't just ask you in a wimpy way, "Well, if you want to and if it's convenient and comfortable, try not to be a full-blown materialist." No, God says, "Don't pursue comfort and material things." Pursue higher values—God's values—*first,* and if wealth comes to you in the process, share it with others and carefully spend it.

Start now to be less of a materialist. Ask God to help you. There may be a day when it *will be* too late to learn how to share with others, to live on less. Set high goals for your life, but not high goals for owning everything under the sun you want.

By holding loosely to things in life, you'll find a new kind of freedom from peer pressure. And you'll also find a great joy from sharing what you have with others.

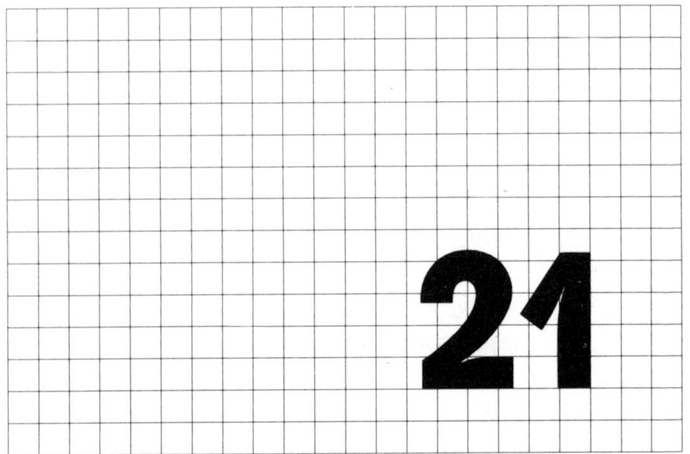

You notice how depressing the evening news is on TV. For 29 minutes, Dan Rather and all his buddies assault you with the lousiest, most depressing stories you can imagine. And then for one minute at the end of their broadcast, they close with some cute little story that is supposed to make you laugh and send you on your way thinking life is wonderful.

Sometimes the news leaves you with a sort of empty feeling that makes you wonder if God has this thing under control, anyway. But more than that, it makes you wonder where you fit in—and if there is a place where you can make a difference in a world gone crazy.

Well, contrary to the evening news, consider this next important starting point.

STARTING POINT 21

You CAN make a difference!

Everyone wonders now and then whether a difference can be made in life. After all, it's a big country and an even bigger world. What can you possibly do to put a dent into the world's problems? It's sort of like voting. Hardly any election is ever lost by just one vote. But yet, everybody says we ought to vote.

Consider your social studies class. It's one problem after another. Poverty hanging on in the inner city, steel mills closing down, teenagers committing suicide, millions of little kids starving to death in Africa, and nuclear power plants burning up. Our world seems to be in a terrible mess, doesn't it?

Can you, with your face, your brain, your hands, your feet, your family background, your past mistakes, come to the party called *life* and make a difference?

The answer is yes.

Not only can you make a difference, but the world—God's world—needs what you've got.

That's right. God's world needs what you've got. God needs you even though you can't dribble a basketball, take a decent picture, or think your way through the first theorem in plane geometry. God can use you to make a difference right where you live. In the house where you live. On your street. In your town. In your school. You can do big things that will make a difference.

One thirty-minute newscast each night can never tell you all the good things that people did that day. In fact, TV, radio, and newspapers thrive on conflict. (Visual, emotional events make "good television.") They thrive on telling you the dark side, because that is what gets people's interest.

But that's not really a balanced picture of our world. When it seems like the whole world is fighting, starving, sleeping around, or catching AIDS, you feel like you can't make a difference, like life is hopeless. But God *does* have the world under His control, and life *isn't* all problems. Sure, there are big problems in the world, but every vote, every dollar, every minute you invest makes a difference.

All those little efforts, the little favors you do for your mom, or the kindnesses you do for your dad, add up to make the world a better place to live in. In today's world, because there are so many problems, it takes a lot of people doing a lot of good deeds and a lot of people reaching out to make the world a better place.

Do you remember one of our first starting points at the beginning of the book? It went like this, "Like it or not, God's in charge." That's comforting to know when you see so much trouble around. But more than comforting, that starting point says that when you know Christ personally, He's in charge of your life. That makes you different. That makes you able to see the world differently. And that also means, according to the Bible, that God gave you some special gifts.

When you came to know Christ, God put in you special gifts and talents which means you can do certain things well in life. You can use each one of those gifts and talents to bring some good into someone's life.

Let's talk about how you can use your talents to make a difference right where you are.

If you are a jock, you can move furniture around some Saturday for your parents or a neighbor. You can make a special effort to protect some little person who is always getting picked on at school.

If you are a computer whiz, you can help in an office somewhere, maybe your parents'.

If you have extra time on your hands, you can babysit or do a summer missions project. You know how summers go. The first couple of weeks are like a dream with no homework to do. Then you start to get bored. You end up hanging out downtown or cruising. Now, that's not the most productive way to spend your time in the summer.

By doing a summer mission's project or doing something with your time to help someone else, you can make a difference right where you are.

Hey, here's a tough one. How about making a difference with some of your money? Buy your dad a car wash, take your mom out for a free lunch, or how about just giving some extra money to the church next week?

If you want to be free from the power that money has on your life, try giving it away. You will find real freedom in giving away some of what you've got. (But don't be too crazy about it—save a little money for a Big Mac and fries next weekend.)

Here's another way to make a difference. Do something in secret. How about trying to do some nice thing for your parents that no one will see but you and God? Or how about saying one prayer every day this week for someone you know who is hurting? No one will ever see those things, but each time you do some kindness for someone and do it in secret, you're making a difference in the world.

You can do all these things with your gifts, your time, your money, and they all make a difference in the world. But what's the ultimate you could do to make a difference in somebody's life? What's the biggest thing you could do with what you've got?

The greatest thing you can do to make a differ-ence in this world is to share with others what Jesus Christ can do. That sounds simple enough on paper, doesn't it? But you know how hard it is in school to stand up for Christ. It's tough to take a stand for what you believe. Yet telling others about Jesus Christ is perhaps the greatest way you can make a long-term difference in life.

How often can or should you do that? Hey, when

God gives you an opportunity, take it. Maybe you need to consider a career of sharing Christ with others as a minister or a missionary. You could use your talents full-time to help some mission or church.

In a very cosmic and preplanned way, God has strategically placed hurting people in your life so you could tell them how good it is to know Jesus Christ. Christ doesn't have any other way to get His Word out to them but you. Quite honestly, if you sit on it and never share what it means to know Christ, you won't make much of a lasting difference in life.

Sure, maybe you'll find the cure for cancer or AIDS and that cure will remove a lot of suffering in the world. You can die knowing you helped a lot of hurting people. But in the end, if you had an opportunity to tell your neighbor or friend that Jesus Christ is the real answer to life's cancers and you didn't do it, then you would have missed the mark.

One of the first Christians, Peter, wrote a letter once to some friends, and here is what he told them:

> Each one should use whatever gift he has received to serve others, faithfully administering God's grace in its various forms. If anyone speaks, he should do it as one speaking the very words of God. If anyone serves, he should do it with the strength God provides, so that in all things God may be praised through Jesus Christ.
>
> —1 PETER 4:10–11 NIV

Those verses say it all. *Make a difference by using whatever gifts and talents you've got to show God's love in various ways.*

This starting point can save you from a boring summer, even a boring life. If you don't put it into place in your life, you'll end up wasting a lot of time focusing on what's hip, the latest clothes you supposedly need, or what movie you should go see.

Hey, stop and think for a minute. There *is* life after high school. In a few years you are going to be out of high school and on to something else in life. But if you never believe you can make a difference, you'll spend your whole life living for yourself. And you know what that means. Zip contribution to this world.

God has a better idea. He says that every time you help someone, you can make a difference. Every time you show love, faith, or justice, it counts. Every time you share the importance of knowing Christ with someone else, you make *ultimate* difference.

Lots of people your age feel that life is hopeless. Some of them put bullets in their head or OD on drugs because they feel they can do nothing to change the world. It's too bad. They believe the evening news. But because you know Christ, you know different. You know the evening news is just a part of the story. Because of Christ there *is* always hope. Go share some of that hope with others and you *will* make a difference in your world.

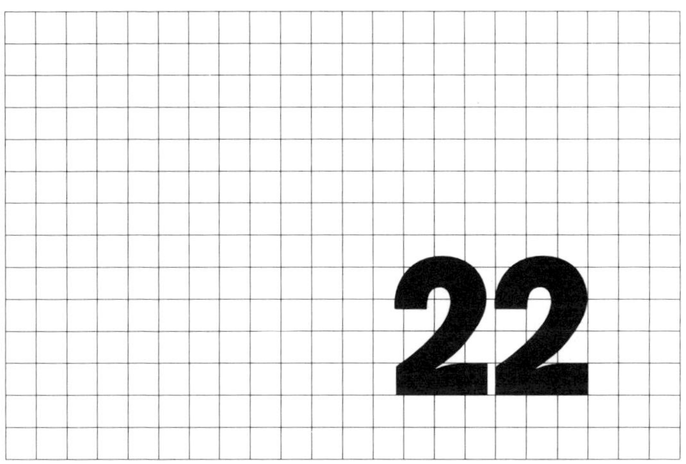

22

Beginning a few years ago, everyone got into the "aid" thing. There was Live Aid, Farm Aid, Band Aid, Sports Aid, Hands Across America, Feet Across Utah, Lawyers Aid, Tennis Elbow Aid. You name it. If someone needed help, somebody else got together a bunch of sports stars and rock stars to hype the cause so people would give to it. Did you ever wonder, though, after the cameras went home and the stage came down, how much help really went to people? And look at the people around you that got involved in those projects. How many would you say really cared about helping somebody else?

So often in life, the people we respect the most are the ones we are the closest to who did something or gave up something important for us. A retiring pro football player once said, "I just want to be remembered for being a good husband and a good father. All the yards gained, all the possessions, all the long passes are history." That retiring football player has a good idea. In fact, he has God's idea. And that brings us to one of our last starting points. Maybe one of the most important ones for you.

STARTING POINT 22

You'll gain your life by losing it.

Jesus really had a radical idea. He talked about it a lot. Once He said, "For whoever wants to save his life will lose it, but whoever loses his life for me and for the gospel will save it" (Mark 8:35 NIV). Another time He told His disciple friends, "If anyone wants to be first, he must be the very last, and the servant of all" (Mark 9:35 NIV).

Jesus told the story about a man beaten and left for dead by robbers. (See Luke 10:25–37.) They took his clothes and his money and left him half dead. Two people passed him by. One was a priest. But a third man, a Samaritan (the kind of person Jews hated and generally thought was scum), came along and acted like a real neighbor and gave help to the man. He gave him first aid and put him in a hotel and paid all the expenses. After Jesus told that story He asked the people who were listening, "Which one of these three do you think was a neighbor to the man who fell into the hands of the robbers?" One lawyer replied, "The one who had mercy on him." And then do you know what Jesus said to him? "Go and do likewise."

That Samaritan gained something big in his life that day by giving up his time and money. He could have blown the guy off, but he didn't. And that was Jesus' idea. *You win when you give.*

No one really seems to think that way today except, of course, Mother Teresa. (And we can all see where that got her. She is not exactly the most wealthy or comfortable person in the world. Or is she?)

Maybe right now it's all you can do to keep your room clean, your grades up, and your parents off your back. And God expects you to find *more* time in your day to do something nice for someone else? It doesn't make sense. People around you probably are grabbing all they can, looking to collect more stuff and things, looking for position and power in life.

That lifestyle runs headlong into conflict with what Jesus said. He said that you'll gain your life through losing it. What's the real truth? Could Christ possibly have meant what He said? Can that possibly make sense in today's world?

Yes, it still makes sense in today's world.

People who leave their mark in life are givers, not takers. They are people who have found a way to be happy in taking a smaller piece of meat on the plate or giving up some time on Saturdays to cut the grass for their dad or mom. They are people who help their brothers or sisters when they'd rather be cruising with friends.

Have you discovered anything like that in your life? Some day the world, your friends, and even God, will look at you and judge you by whether you were generous or tight with what you had in life. Maybe you feel really busy right now. School is too much, and you've got your own goals that require more of your time.

So here's the radical part of Jesus' idea. Even when you've got a lot going, when you empty yourself and give of your time and efforts to other people, you gain something. You feel worthwhile, rich, and alive. That's hard to believe. But you can experience this kind of well-being, too, by being determined to be more of a giver than a taker. Being more of a giver than a taker looks like this:

- Leaving your girlfriend's or boyfriend's dignity and morals intact, even if you get a little hot.
- Controlling your temper.
- Volunteering for a job at church.
- Holding the door for someone at school.
- Not barging to be first in line.
- Praying for someone faithfully.
- Settling for the small piece of pizza without complaining.

- Not falling asleep when your sister or brother is telling you a big problem.
- Sharing your jeans without complaining.
- Setting your sights on God's goals, not your own.

It's part of God's plan for you.

Remember when Scrooge woke up on Christmas Eve? He had tons of money and no friends. No personal growth. No happiness. And he was very much alone in life.

Scrooge is still alive in today's world.

One reason why so many people turn to cocaine and alcohol may be because sex with thirty people and a nice car left them empty inside. They were looking out for themselves, and in the end they found it didn't pay off at all.

Jesus' idea absolutely contradicts everything you hear today and everything our culture says you have a right to "enjoy." His idea may not always feel good or be comfortable, but it is right. *You gain the best things in life by giving your life to others.*

Many teenagers are looking for a sense of purpose. They are looking for joy and happiness. They want to experience highs. They want to know God in a new way. They want to have a lot of friends and feel secure and not have a lot of hassles with authority. Do you want those things?

The path to all those things is giving your life away. It's going the extra mile, being kind to others who are different from yourself.

Want to feel that life is worth living? Put this starting point in place in your life. It'll pay big dividends the rest of your life.

God didn't give you your hands and feet to sit on. Get yourself involved. Give what you've got away, and God will give you a rich, full life.

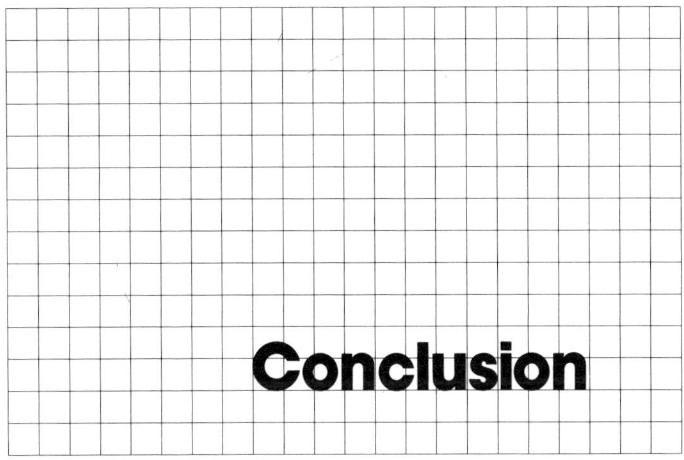

Conclusion

So, here we are down to the last chapter. Each of the starting points you've been reading about is like a computer command on an F-16 aircraft. To get that big jet off the ground, computers on board have to be programmed correctly or that jet won't take off. It's the same with the space shuttle. To get off the launch pad, every space shuttle needs a good start, a good boost, or it goes nowhere. Well, that's what this book has been all about. Starting points are takeoff points found in the Bible to boost your experience of God's very best for you.

Sometimes, though, we tend to think that we can run our own life just fine. If we're smart and healthy, it's easy to simply drift away and not really count on God for anything. Then when trouble hits, we make a mess because we counted on our own strength to get us through. That's when we fail and have sex when we shouldn't or cheat on a test or really mess up at home. And that's when we need God to come in and comfort us and forgive us and put us back on our feet and get us started again on the right path to give us the hope He promised.

Tomorrow, the next day, and the next year, you are going to be confronted with a lot of decisions in your life. What college to attend? What person to date? What career to choose? How pure to be on a date? That's when you need God, and that's when these starting points are going to be important in your life.

Two thousand years ago, James, a wise servant of God, gave some good advice to some friends. Here it is:

> Do not merely listen to the word, and so deceive yourselves. Do what it says. Anyone who listens to the word but does not do what it says is like a man who looks at his face in a mirror and, after looking at himself, goes away and immediately forgets what he looks like. But the man who looks intently into the perfect law that gives freedom, and continues to do this, not forgetting what he has heard, but doing it—he will be blessed in what he does.
>
> —JAMES 1:22–25 NIV

James gave good advice, and it applies to you.

In this book you've read about getting important starts in life in a lot of key areas, but if you throw the book away and don't do what these starting points say, you're going to miss what these starting points promise—and that's freedom. Freedom from bad ideas about God. Freedom from bad ideas the world gives you about sex and being truthful. Freedom from fear and uncertainty and boredom.

If you want to experience life at its very best, put these starting points—every one of them—to work in your life. When you forget them, go back and re-read them. And **if you ever find that you've lost your way or need a new start, stop and check God's Word.**

Go and be a friend of God's, and you will find that God will be a friend to you. **You can count on the God of good starts and new starts to be there to guide you.** His plan, your effort. His laws, your will. His dreams, your life.

From your good friend who has come to know that God's starting points are best,